6531

SPLENDOUR
from
THE SEA

13 V

W. Phillip Keller

SPLENDOUR
from
THE SEA

THE SAGA OF
THE SHANTYMEN

MOODY PRESS
CHICAGO

TO
THOSE SHANTYMEN
WHOSE FIELD IS
"THE GRAVEYARD OF THE PACIFIC"

*"They that go down to the sea in ships,
that do business in great waters;
These see the works of the Lord, and
his wonders in the deep."*

PSALM 107:23-24

Acknowledgements

MY GENUINE GRATITUDE must be expressed, first of all, to "The Shanty Boys" themselves, who not only shared their homes, boats and equipment with me, but also their own personal lives.

For those photographs marked *LIFE,* sincere thanks go to *LIFE* magazine of New York, who so kindly put these prints at my disposal.

The generosity of the British Columbia Government, in allowing me access to various photographic files, from which some of the illustrations have been drawn, is hereby acknowledged.

Mr. R. Langshaw of Trochu, Alberta was most helpful and gracious in the preparation of my own photographs.

The encouragement of Mr. T. S. Rendall, who read the rough draft, was a vital inspiration to the work.

The attractive line drawings were graciously executed, upon my suggestion, by the late Mrs. J. Thompson of Salt Spring Island—another friend of the Shantymen.

To my family, who listened patiently to the narration, as I read it to them for comment, I owe a special word of appreciation.

Finally I feel deeply indebted to all those who have prayed that this project might be a credit to the cause of Christ.

THE AUTHOR

Table of Contents

Photographs

11

To You Who Read

THE WARMTH AND SOFTNESS of late summer hung in a blue sky that arched itself over the equally blue water of the Pacific. Tiny breaths of wind riffled the surface of the straits that lay tranquil and contented between the southern tip of Vancouver Island and the rock ridges of the Olympic Peninsula in Washington.

Into the shimmering waters of a narrow channel that ran amidst the rocks and islands just offshore in these Straits of Juan de Fuca, a trim white boat nosed her way cautiously—as though feeling for safe footing in the treacherous pass.

The motors idled gently to a stop; the vessel drifted momentarily; then the rattle of an anchor chain whose anchor found a hold on the rocks, bringing it to a halt—held against the running current of the ebb tide.

On a low rise of grassy ground above the shore stood a tiny white cottage—built of driftwood planks and boards that had been gathered from the storm-lashed beaches and bays that dotted this Rocky Point. Out of this little, lonely house dashed a tiny girl, starry-eyed with excitement at the sight of the glistening white craft that had dropped anchor in her "front yard."

Her father, too, a young man, brown and burned with sun and wind on his wild acres of sheep range, straightened from his work in the turnip field, shading his eyes with a horny hand to watch what was happening on the boat.

Across the water came the chatter of lighthearted voices—stray snatches of tunes and the clatter of men getting into a dinghy to row themselves ashore. By this time the young mother's curiosity, too, was aroused and soon all three of the family stood on the beach waiting to welcome the strangers.

13

As the dinghy grated on the gravel—the rancher reached out a hand to help it ashore—and with the other grasped the strong hand of a man who was destined to become one of his finest friends . . . a Shantyman.

Before the western sun had settled in splendour behind the ragged conifers on the skyline—the two Shanty boys from the boat had bent their backs to the long rows of turnips and finished the tedious task that the rancher had begun alone in the morning.

That evening the little driftwood cabin was aglow with the warmth of happy hearts content in each other's company. The room was pungent with the aroma of a venison stew—and a small girl's gentle giggles rippled across the room from where she sat curled up in the brawny arms of the Shantyman who but a few hours before had been a total stranger to her.

It was late that night—when, after a simple reading of the Scriptures and the sharing of some songs—the boys took their leave again. Out they went into the pungent darkness of the Pacific night—out onto the broad waters of the swelling ocean whose waves lapped this rugged West Coast of Vancouver Island—out onto the field of service where their lives were lived for the glory of God and the service of their fellowmen.

That was fifteen years ago—and that wee girl was my daughter. The intervening years have been marked with a deepening friendship for these men—the Shantymen—and an ever greater esteem for their practical yet radiant demonstration of God's faithfulness to mankind.

Out of a sincere sense of affection and regard for those missionaries on the "Graveyard of the Pacific" this narrative has been written.

No attempt has been made in this book to deal with the whole far-flung Shantymen's work of North America that stretches from coast to coast. Instead only that part of it directly related to Vancouver Island, with which I am intimately acquainted, has been covered.

In essence the West Coast is a unique field of service whose closest counterpart would be Sir Wilfred Grenfell's well-known

Labrador enterprise. All of the same basic elements are there: the rugged, forbidding coastline; the angry seas; the tough breed of men who make this their home; the small, sturdy boats of the missionaries; the warm, enduring compassion of strong men called of God to minister to both the hearts and bodies of tough people in tough places.

Yet over and beyond an honest desire to portray the Shantymen's splendid service in its finest form, there lies deep within these pages an impulse more profound. Put in simple language it is: to demonstrate the great and unchanging trustworthiness of God Himself.

In writing on any theme connected with Christian endeavour a layman sails in difficult waters. Ever present, close to the surface of his conscience, there lie the reefs of temptation which would have him extol the personalities of his leading characters. There are, too, the crosscurrents of conflict in his mind as to how much emphasis should be placed on the planning, the programmes, the policies, the people involved in such an enterprise.

In order to steer a safe course through these seas, great pains have been taken to keep this account simple and straightforward, centered on the compass-bearing of God's unfailing goodness to men.

This point was made very clear to all those who were interviewed while gathering the material for this work. It is a measure of their stature that every individual agreed wholeheartedly to the suggestion that above all else it was to God that honour should be given—not to themselves.

Living as we do in an era of history when men well nigh worship man himself as though he were God—because of his scientific achievements—it is refreshing to find simple humble men like these "Shanty Boys" through whom God still demonstrates to mortals His own irrevocable power and presence in everyday living.

Should anyone doubt the validity of what I have just written I would challenge them to spend two weeks on board "Messenger III"—living and working with these men in action. And

I make bold to say they would have to admit—"God is here"—and feel humbled because of it.

At the suggestion of the Shantymen themselves, their own proper names have been omitted from the narrative—instead synonyms have been used—whereby anyone, even though only casually acquainted with their work, will immediately recognize them.

To write a carefully documented account of the life of any single member of this group would in itself consume a book. Furthermore it would be utterly impossible to tell of all the wondrous work God has accomplished in this field without going to several volumes.

There has fallen upon me, therefore, the responsibility of relating those episodes which I deemed essential to the body of the book. The order and sequence in which these have been arranged are also my work. In this, author's license has been exercised in order to produce a continuous story that anyone might follow with ease. Nevertheless, no effort has been spared to keep the narrative as accurate as possible and in the closest chronological order feasible.

If the pages that follow warm your heart towards God our Father for His enduring faithfulness—if they urge you to give more of yourself to Him for His service—if they make you proud to be His child—then they will have been well worth writing.

More than this though—they have purposely been written in simple, ordinary, layman's language, in order that anyone might read them with complete understanding. If in that understanding, there falls upon someone's heart the awareness that they too wish to know God—to love Him and to trust Him more wholeheartedly—it will have been doubly worth doing.

THE AUTHOR
(A friend of the Shanty Boys)

West Coast Seascape

W. Phillip Keller

A Lonely Lighthouse

W. Phillip Keller

In "The Graveyard of the Pacific"

Men and Material Come Ashore

The Graveyard of the Pacific

A T LEAST TEN YEARS of my own life have been lived continuously on the edge of "The Graveyard of the Pacific"—a common name given to the wild and broken coastline of western Vancouver Island. For me that has been "home" and though I am not a mariner I have sailed through its storm-lashed waters, and stood often upon its shore which trembled under the impact of furious weather.

In order that the reader should appreciate more fully the atmosphere and environment of this coast; in order that he should grasp its rugged character and picture in his mind the stern setting in which most of the events in this book took place, I have taken it upon myself to describe a fragment of this winding, deeply indented shoreline that reaches from Race Rocks on the southernmost tip of the Island to Cape Scott at its northern extremity.

Unless one can see the dark grey seas driven by tempestuous winds, mounting to foaming white crests that roll landward to charge rank on rank against the black reefs and drab headlands; unless one can taste the tang of salt spray and spume carried on the scudding air that whips it into the stunted timber and scrubby brush that grip the shore; unless one can sense the drip of endless rain on rotting leaves or sodden trees; un-

19

less one can smell the iodine aroma of seaweed under the sun and hear the plaintive cries of seagulls wheeling in the wind, these pages can scarcely come alive.

There are perhaps few areas of coastline, of comparable length, anywhere on earth, which have taken as great a toll of men and ships as has this violent strand. From the exciting records of adventuresome men, audacious enough to venture near its reefs, or anxious to probe its inlets, there has flowed a continuous series of shipwrecks and disaster. Not a year passes without its toll of sunken craft and lost lives.

Yet in spite of its grim visage; in spite of its wicked weather; in spite of its savage storms; in spite of its remoteness and comparative isolation, the West Coast continues to lure men to herself. Some are drawn there for the rich harvest of fish from the sea—for the salmon and herring; the halibut and cod— yes, even the whales. Other men have been attracted by the great stands of timber that make some of them rich and that drive others under the heel of bankruptcy. Minerals too have cast their glittering enchantment upon men's minds and brought them from the far corners of the Commonwealth to creep through the dense salal and climb the rock ridges searching for elusive wealth that seems always to lurk just over the next hill.

A few tough settlers, too, have tramped out a trail to some silt-laden valley—daring to hew out for themselves a small kingdom of open ground from a terrible tangle of gigantic stumps and dank undergrowth. Though they may have found their freedom—it is only by a continuous battle with the surrounding woodland growth that they can hold their little kingdom against the pressing forest which waits relentlessly to march its cohorts across their fields, claiming them again for itself.

Besides these, there are, too, a slim scattering of service personnel, lighthouse keepers, fur trappers, tradesmen, fire fighters and other sundry officials whose lot has been cast upon this shore.

Hovering darkly in the background—yet as ever present as the dense shadows of the fir forests—are the Indians—scattered at random up and down the inlets in their grey wooden shacks. Of these the great majority cling to their past history—hoping as if by some miracle—there might suddenly emerge from the grey mists of time a shaman who would or could deliver them from the poverty of their present existence. Meanwhile they shuffle along the sodden trails that lead from weather-beaten shack to weather-beaten shack—hunched against the rain, backs to the breeze, hoping that tomorrow might just happen to be not quite as bad as today.

This then is the "Graveyard of the Pacific"—its landscape and its people. This is the field of endeavour in which the Shantymen do their work. This is the rough forbidding world into which they come—with God.

Amongst those to whom they minister—as in every work—there are some who welcome them with open doors and a hearty handshake. But by the same measure there are those who despise their cause and spurn the God they serve. Then in betwixt the two lie that great mass of the indifferent, uncommitted ones.

Andy was one such. One of those who neither cared nor thought of his destiny as long as he had grub and smokes enough for today.

He was the lightkeeper on the Race Rocks light, whose beam stretched its long yellow finger through our own cottage window each night—as it rotated slowly in its long steady swing through 360 degrees.

Between us and that tall tower marked boldly in black and white rings stretched several miles of angry, dangerous water. Even in midsummer on a dead calm day the rip tides would surge and churn between the race rocks and our point of land until they were foaming white and roaring with the frenzy of raging whitecaps.

Getting supplies on and off that rock for the lightkeeper, his family and his assistant was a risky game. Andy's predecessor had been a careful, cautious man who rarely ever lingered at our dock more than a moment to say "Hello" lest the tides change and cut off his return.

But Andy was of a different stamp. He was a daring, dashing Cockney, who had flown countless bomber raids over Berlin and who laughed in the teeth of danger. Whenever he came to our side, he always seemed to have time to drink a cup of tea, chat a while, and yarn about his colourful career. Meanwhile the sea might be making up into a boiling froth. Nonchalantly he would loose his small white boat from the dock, head her into the waves with his tam pulled down at a jaunty angle to the wind, and wave farewell with a grin creasing his face.

One Christmas Eve, in spite of the storm warnings, Andy came ashore for his Christmas mail and supplies. I had cut a Christmas tree for him to take back to the "Rock" to cheer his children. We loaded in his packages, covered them securely with a tarpaulin, and planted the little pine jauntily at the bow of his small white boat.

While we were storing his stuff, the wind was making up and a touch of snow was on its breath. I urged him to come into our cottage and wait out the storm—but he was insistent that he would go in spite of the blow.

Perhaps in his mind's eye there were visions of candlelight and Christmas ornaments on the tree that night in his home on the rock. Perhaps he saw letters from London and bulging parcels opened by his excited youngsters. Perhaps the thought of roast turkey, plum pudding and a waiting woman standing at the window peering through the gloom for signs of his small white boat goaded him on.

At any rate Andy started his motor. It coughed and ran rough—giving me an uneasy feeling. Again I held the lines—reluctant to cut him loose into the tide. But he was determined to leave.

By this time snow was heavy on the rising wind—gusting across the ground in sheets of blinding whiteness. Andy swung his boat into the tide. As it struck the waves the little Christmas tree bounced merrily at its pitching bow. There was one final wave of his arm and the storm blotted him from my sight as he headed into the waste of wild water.

That was the last moment anyone ever saw him. For nearly

ten days a frantic woman and weeping youngsters awaited his return . . . . in vain.

We combed the coast line of rugged rock and log-littered bays for his body but it was never found. "The Graveyard of the Pacific" had taken its toll once more.

It is amid such wild settings of stormy seas, wind-lashed trees, and broken rock that this book has been born.

Laying a Foundation

IT IS AN ESSENTIAL PART of God's plan for any man or woman who is to be of service in His cause that they be adequately trained and thoroughly prepared for the purpose to which He calls them. This period of preparation—this time of laying the foundation for future work—is often an arduous and rigorous experience for the individual. Nonetheless God, knowing as He does the end from the beginning, does not hesitate to put His chosen ones into tormenting situations and testing trials. This He does not only to prove to them His own great trustworthiness—but also to purify their characters, to temper the strength of their trust in Himself, and to whet the keenness of their witness through depending on His own infallible Word.

As the leading characters of this story are introduced into the work of the Shantymen, where they play a prominent part, a little of their background will be recounted. This will help the reader to appreciate that these are, after all, very ordinary men—called of God—taught of Himself—tested by His appointment that they might become useful individuals in the work of His kingdom on earth.

For the stern and demanding life of Shantymen missionaries on the West Coast—God saw fit to select men of strong physical stamina—pioneer stock—rugged individualism and adventurous spirit. Still over and beyond these natural attributes He knew they would need a strong spiritual life, a dynamic power in their personalities that had its origin in Himself. That is why in every case a solid foundation of personal experiences, in which God demonstrated His power to provide for any situation, was laid in their lives before ever they became active on the coast.

So it was that ten years before he was called to join the Shantymen, a young backwoods missionary in the far northerly bush country of Alberta was being equipped and trained for service by God. For him those pioneer years were desperately hard on the body—for he was having to learn to die to his own desires. In the spirit, however, they were years of exultation and triumph as daily he found his spirit renewed within him.

This young man who had, before his conversion, known only the hard-drinking, fast-money, barrack-toughened life of the army, gave himself unreservedly to God's service. He moved into the north country as an unpaid backwoods missionary . . . determined to live what is sometimes called a "life of faith." This latter is a somewhat confusing term for it refers to anyone who entrusts all their earthly needs to God's care, believing that He is able to provide for them in every situation—on the proviso that they themselves are entirely and irrevocably committed to God's work and cause. It has no bearing upon the word *faith* in the usual sense of a creed, dogma or belief to which a group of people may subscribe.

For the young missionary this life of faith became a tormenting and perplexing enigma early in his career. That first summer he survived in a shack on little more than wheat and eggs. Unaccustomed to the tough life of the northern frontier he had arrived there totally ignorant of how to live in a climate where the appalling blizzards and frigid temperatures of winter made life impossible for anyone not properly equipped to meet them.

This became painfully apparent as the first fall season arrived and he found himself without adequate clothing to prevent usual frost-bites. So the question entered his mind—"Am

I to continue to try and merely live by faith in God—or shall I
choose the course of finding work?"

Finally in this dilemma of a divided mind, on a frosty autumn
morning he threw himself on his knees before God praying—
"Oh, God, you know I have need of clothes. If it is your wish
that I should work and earn the money for them—reveal your
will this day. If someone offers me a job today I will accept this
as your provision for my need."

That very morning a great burly Swede came pounding on his
door. "Will you come work for me?" he boomed in broken English. "My threshing crew is shorthanded. I need another man."

Only as long as it took to change into his overalls did the
young missionary detain the farmer. Then away they went
to the giant steam-driven threshing outfit where sixteen teams
spewed a continuous river of golden sheaves into the mighty
maw of the machine.

He was assigned the job of spike pitcher, feeding the monster
machine—a back breaking, killing job that at the end of four
days almost had the unhardened fellow flat with fatigue. By a
miracle it rained the fifth day. During this rainy spell his
strength was rejuvenated. His young muscles hardened like
those of a fighting cock. From then until the end of the season
he worked with eager zest and unflinching determination, even
though some of the days stretched out late into the northern
night when straw stacks were set alight so that the crews could
see to keep working.

Then the season ended and he drew his wage, which in those
days was the fabulous sum of eight dollars a day. Immediately
he sent away for warm clothing to outfit himself for winter.
At the same time a crafty salesman approached the crew in
camp soliciting orders on heavy sheepskin-lined coats, for each
of which he collected forty-five dollars in cash from the un-
suspecting men. With this haul in hand the man disappeared—
never to be seen again. The enraged men summoned the police
who asked the missionary if he too had lost some money. "No,"
he replied—for to him this was God's money—not his. If God
had given it—He was also entitled to take it from him. This was

a lesson not many men that young learn quite so readily. Somehow he felt confident that if he bore this loss or any other loss—even that of his personal reputation—with patience and serenity, God Himself would in due course more than reimburse him for it.

It was several weeks later that one Saturday night while preparing his talks for the next day, there came a knock at his cabin door. A man stood there with a large bulky parcel which had been shipped from a mail-order house.

"A parcel for you, sir!"

"Not for me," the missionary replied. "I didn't order anything from that company."

"Well it's addressed to you—here, take it!" and it was thrust into his hands.

With bewilderment he took it inside and with excited, trembling fingers tore open the package.

Inside was a magnificent warm fur coat—far better than anything he might have bought himself.

God had truly vindicated Himself beyond measure.

                     o   o   o

The missionary's unfamiliarity with this untamed northland extended beyond not knowing just how to dress for the weather or contend with its vicious elements. The tangle of uncharted little narrow trails which wound their way through the bush country had to become his highways over which he traveled countless miles on foot with a pack, visiting from homestead to homestead—from isolated community to logging camp to lonely hamlet. So it is not altogether surprising that on occasion he became lost and in danger of losing life itself.

One bright sunny morning he set off in high spirits to visit a small place called Red Cross, where a group of settlers had invited him to come and minister to them. He had only packed two light blankets for his trip, omitting to put matches, knife or hatchet in his knapsack, since he felt confident he would reach his destination in good time if he set a fast pace on the trail.

He started out in the frosty, sparkling morning sunlight, following the indistinct trail where only one or two sleighs had

passed sometime before. As the day progressed ominous dark
clouds gathered overhead and a chill cutting wind began to
blow from the northwest.

With a sudden intensity for which northern blizzards are
famous, a storm engulfed him. He found himself floundering
along, trying desperately to follow the tracks which were becoming more and more obscured by the falling snow and
ground drift. It was not long until he realized that he was no
longer on the trail, but wandering aimlessly in the thickening
darkness of a blizzard and hopelessly lost.

To roll up in the two blankets he carried would be fatal, for
already most of his strength had been sapped and the plunging
temperature dropping deep below zero would soon snuff out
his life. He began to reel with weakness while that fuzzy sense
of inertia which descends over the brain in mercy before a freez-
ing death hovered in his mind.

Exhausted he slumped behind a stump and committed his
soul to God—fully prepared to accept any lot that befell him.

He had scarcely done this when he thought he detected the
sound of wagon wheels.

"Wagon wheels!" he ejaculated in his dazed state. "Wagon
wheels in the snow—surely not!"

Again the sound came; more clearly this time. In desperation
he rallied himself and tried to stagger towards it.

He stumbled out to a small knoll and there sure enough he
thought he could detect a team coming out of the driving snow
toward him. He shouted at the top of his lungs.

There was a "Whoa!" and the team stopped.

The farmer leaped from his sleigh and came over to gather
him up—bundling him into the deep bedded straw in the bottom
of the sleigh box. Behind the sleigh sure enough there was
tied another team pulling an empty lumber wagon with its log
bunkers. So he had heard wagon wheels—and by a miracle had
been rescued.

The farmer gave the horses their head and soon the two
chilled men arrived at a little logging camp. The owner—a tall

broad-built man with two months' growth of beard upon his face—came out to meet them.

"Who is this you've got with you?" he shouted, tobacco juice dribbling down over his grizzled beard.

"If it's a hunter he's more than welcome!"

"Yes, I'm a hunter alright!" the missionary replied, "I've come up to look for men, to tell them of Christ the Saviour, who has changed my life!"

"Well," the logger bellowed, "at least it's a change to meet someone up here who can talk about things other than trees and timber!"

The lumberman invited him over to his cabin, and on the way they passed the cookhouse. Tacked to the door was a notice: "Meals—40¢ cash!" The missionary put his hand in his pocket. The solitary silver quarter lying there felt mighty inadequate to a young man chilled and half-starved.

In the lumberman's cabin there were two cots and he was invited to use one. In a few moments the logger shouted for his flunky and ordered him to bring two full suppers to the cabin. They would dine in style!

How good God was!

The two men talked all through the meal. They talked on till midnight—they talked on into the small hours of the morning—they talked on until five o'clock when suddenly the logger said, "I want to accept Christ Jesus as my Lord and my Saviour!"

What a transformation there was in that heart.

"How wonderful if my wife knew of this!" he exclaimed.

"Where is your wife?" the missionary enquired eagerly.

"Twenty-six miles back in the direction you came from!" was the answer.

"Then certainly I'll hit the trail again to find her, even if it's the opposite way to which I was going."

Out into the snow and ice the young pastor plunged the next day, fighting his way down the trail looking for the logger's wife.

As dusk approached he found it necessary to drop in at a strange farmhouse and seek shelter for the night. To his joy—but also to his questioning—he found these farmer folk to be most hospitable but of a different religious persuasion.

Oh, yes, they loved the Lord—they loved God's Word—but—a big *but*—they weren't the same denomination as he. So doubtful and painful misgivings entered his heart. "Could he enjoy their fellowship?"

That night as they read the Bible together—as they warmed their hearts in prayer—as they spoke of the God they loved—there came into the young man's awareness that in Christ all men are brothers. And from that night divisions of doctrine or denomination carried little weight with him.

As it happened this elderly couple turned out to be the parents of the logger's wife, whom he sought. So together they went gladly to her home near at hand the next day. There they met her, and the missionary again discussed the wonders of God's Word.

Before the sun had set, not only had this woman but also her two children, given their allegiance to Christ. How great was the joy in the home of those dear old folks to see their daughter and grandchildren so transformed.

That night as he looked back over the events of the past two days there was impressed deeply on this young man's mind the concept that God uses the most adverse and sometimes baffling circumstances to achieve His purposes. In that knowledge he found fresh strength for all his future!

A Man and a Maid

I T WAS SOME TWO YEARS LATER that another mother lay in bed with her leg broken in three places. The limb had been encased in a heavy plaster cast and was suspended in traction from the ceiling of the room. The injury caused excruciating pain—so hurtful indeed that she was under the watchful care of special nurses day and night, with constant sedation.

Into this setting there stepped the young missionary from the bush country of the northern frontier. He was now a burly, powerful youth who delighted in the strength of his manhood and revelled in the heady joy of life itself. More than this, though, there shone from his face that radiance which is the heritage of those whose hearts are in tune with God.

This forceful character had been chosen—though perhaps it did not then occur to him—in the great providence of God for a life of service to those lonely, scattered remnants of society who find themselves flung out upon the western frontiers of our Pacific Coast . . . the loggers . . . the fishermen . . . the prospectors . . . the ranchers . . . the lighthouse keepers and seamen of assorted kinds.

Yet on this decisive day when he stood quietly beside the bed of this pain-racked woman he was far removed from the wild west coast. Instead he was in the city of Edmonton—bidden to

the side of this woman that he might succour and strengthen
her in her agony of distress. For at this time the missionary was
holding some special meetings in the city.

Humbly and gently he bowed his head—committing to the
tender care of Almighty God the woman in her pain. This was
no idle, empty gesture. Rather it was the expression of an implicit confidence in the power of his Heavenly Father to heal
broken bodies—and mend wounded minds.

Suddenly the woman began to cry out in great excitement,
"I'm healed—I'm healed!"

Such an event came as a shock to the nurse in attendance.
Perhaps never before had she seen so evident a demonstration
of the power of God in her medical career. But the patient, in
her right mind, continued to call out—insisting that she was
able to walk if they would but take off the cast.

The doctor who had cared for the woman was summoned in
haste—himself refusing to believe that such an event could
have occurred. The cast was removed—however—and the patient walked.

Now this lady had a daughter—who though reaching the full
flower of womanhood—was delicate in health and weak in
body. In fact it would be difficult to draw—even in fiction—a
more deliberate contrast than that between this frail city-bred
girl and the burly backwoods missionary.

It was a day or two later that while deep in meditation and
prayer there sprang voluntarily into his conscience the implicit
impression that this girl was to be his wife. Such an assurance
was the more remarkable since he had of his own volition given
his life to God's service as a single man, knowing full well the
terrible sacrifices demanded of any maid wed to a wandering
missionary in the west.

"Me, marry this girl—whom I scarcely have seen, who is a
stranger—a frail fragment of womanhood?"

These and a score of other scorching, searing, probing ques-
tions poured through his mind in tumbled turmoil.

"No, it cannot be—it could never work!"

Yet the impression persisted—nor would it be denied. He simply had to settle the issue by instant and deliberate action.

He found the girl sitting at the piano playing. Boldly—yet in a gentlemanly manner—he sat down on the stool beside her. Without fanfare or emotion he put the question to her bluntly.

"Would you come with me into the mission field?"

The young lady thought only in terms of her music.

"You mean as your accompanist?" she countered.

"No—as my wife."

It was natural that she should be overwhelmed by such a proposal from a man who had never, up to this point, even held her hand.

She hesitated in her reply—as anyone might—when confronted with such a momentous decision for which there had been no previous preparation. "I will have to think about it and pray for guidance."

With that the young man took his leave of the city—not knowing what this woman's decision might be; if anything, torn between two fears—one that she might say "Yes," the other that she might say "No." Either way he was faced with an anxiety common to those in love.

Back to the Northern woods he went—back to the tiny hamlets . . . the scattered settlers . . . the rough men of the North which were his parish.

Three weeks later a wire came for him. It read: "I cannot eat, sleep or work without thinking of you. My answer is 'yes!'"

Thus without courtship—without elaborate preparation of mind or body—God in His infinite wisdom saw fit to draw together this couple who were to become the mainstay of a work He Himself had planned for them long years in advance.

God's ways are not man's ways, nor are His thoughts our thoughts.

It is wonderful that such is the case—for only thus can men adequately entrust their careers to His care.

Had this humble woodsman searched the length of the long Northland for a better bride no doubt he would never have found her. Had he with his own intelligence attempted to choose a helpmate for himself he would undoubtedly have made a mistake in selecting a woman to match his own physical stamina.

Instead in the wondrous provision of God Himself, there was brought to his side a woman, who though weak in body was strong in spirit—endowed with a keen intellect—prepared to share her husband unselfishly with the work to which he was called.

The story of their lives together—the memory of their ministry to men—is fundamentally that of a dynamic man in action at the front, backed unflinchingly by a serene and quiet woman who stands in the background. Only those who have shared in the lonely life of a man or woman separated from their love-mate can appreciate fully the devotion demanded by such a sacrifice. Nevertheless anything worthwhile comes at a great price and this is no less true of Christian service.

Anywhere that gains are made for God, we may be sure it is because someone, somewhere, perhaps unknown—unsung—is paying the price with deliberate self-denial. The mark made by this sturdy missionary in the rough-and-tumble lives of Western folk was that much deeper and more lasting because of the courageous, unseen woman who stood always beside him with her shining spirit. Again and again in later years she would urge him to go out. "Go out to the fields—go out to the forest camps, go out to the lonely fishermen who need you!"

In spite of the feeble frame—in spite of the lonely nights—in spite of the heart tug every time he turned to leave her alone —she urged him on in the work. Are we surprised then that miners and Indians, lumberjacks and fishermen were to find God and a reason for living, under this woodsman? Are we taken back to hear of men being healed and broken homes restored by the touch of the Master—because this humble man moved amongst them? Indeed not! Nor will such wonders of God's mercy to men cease as long as there are behind the scenes those who will die to themselves—that others might live!

Her Crew Are Part of the Boys' Field

"Messenger III" Skirts a Fog Bank

Building a Davis Raft

West Coast Logging Road

A Pioneer Honeymoon

WHEN THE WEDDING DATE ARRIVED, the missionary, attired in an ill-fitting and rather ghastly brown suit that had been purchased in one of the frontier stores, made his way back to the city for his bride.

In his pocket he carried the formidable sum of $15.00, which along with their sincere best wishes, had been the parting gift of his poor parishioners. For in those early days of the North-land money was virtually nonexistent amongst the settlers, most of whom relied on barter to survive.

This $15.00 had already been apportioned in the young man's mind, who fully expected to have a quiet, modest wedding in the bride's home.

Five dollars would pay for the marriage license, $5.00 for the ring, and $5.00 for the preacher.

To his dismay he discovered that elaborate plans had been made for a large reception—hundreds of guests had been invited and quite obviously neither his appearance nor his purse was suited to the occasion. The preacher's wife insisted that he was getting quite one of the finest girls in town, for whom such a drab brown suit simply was not appropriate. Gifts too would have to be procured for some of the attendants, while the church rather than the bride's private home was to be smothered in flowers.

To make him feel even more insecure was the fact that already on the first day of his arrival he found the license would cost $7.50, and the ring was to be $8.50. This he could only leave with the jeweller for engraving by placing a deposit upon it, since his sum of $15.00 had already been exceeded.

That night, deeply distressed in heart and mind, at this sudden—and what he felt was an unfair—turn of events, the young missionary sought God in prayer for long hours. If there was to be a solution to his plight only God could provide it.

The next morning just as he and his fiancée were leaving the house to go downtown in search of a more suitable suit they were met by the postman. He asked if a man of the missionary's name was residing at the girl's home. When told that this was in fact the man, he delivered to him two envelopes, one of which was a government missive marked O.H.M.S. (On His Majesty's Service).

Opening this one first, there fell out a cheque for $100.00—in those days an immense sum. The second letter was from his family and contained a gift of $25.00. By the time the wedding was over that night all the unexpected obligations had been cared for in a hilarious manner. The bride and groom found themselves penniless, however, with only their love left as surety for the unknown future of a frontier life together.

Back to the bush they went, back to the single simple room in an old farmhouse that had been turned over to them as a honeymoon cottage. This by dint of renovation, new paint, and fresh wall paper, the young man had prepared previously as a love nest for his bride.

The first night he found himself unable to sleep. Instead, fingers of fire seemed to place themselves on his skin. The irritation grew worse as he rolled and turned irritably, much to his bride's bewilderment.

Finally in utter exasperation he reared from the bed, struck a match and lit the oil lamp. There upon the sheets moved small brown blobs that had been the cause of his suffering. Why his bride did not get their attention remains a mystery.

The next morning they borrowed a small tent and pitched this under some little poplars in the farmer's yard. There the balance of their honeymoon at the farm was spent in simple bliss.

It was shortly after this that they arranged to hold some major tent meetings on a bald patch of prairie, donated to them for the purpose by a friendly farmer. The site was eight miles from the nearest village—yet word spread by the human telegraph of the North to every homestead and hamlet for a hundred miles or more.

Farm families from far and near came in to attend. Revelling in the comradeship and hearty spirit of the campaign, folks lingered on for days, most of them camped in small tents.

God's mighty power was most apparent in those services and men and women from every age and station of the local populace came under conviction. Many of those who came into a direct and personal relationship with God knew nothing whatever of spiritual terminology or Christian phraseology. Yet their experience was so real and vital as to be positively exhilarating.

One tough cowboy in the ecstasy of his new-found joy leaped up on a bench and waving his ten-gallon stetson excitedly shouted out: "Hurrah for Jesus!"

Four other men, each of them over the age of eighty, also met God in their lives. Late into the night the old-timers would talk about and discuss their new-found joy. Then just as they were retiring, with arms around each other's shoulders, they would bid each other good night with the remark: "Good night, young fellers, we'll see you in the morning."

So it was that as the meeting progressed, the spirit of joy flowed freely and hearts were refreshed and melted under the impact of God's Word.

In response to this, neighbors and farmers from all around gave generously of food and supplies to provide for the sixty to one hundred families that were in attendance.

Late one night, however, the cook who had become a veritable firebrand for God after his conversion a few months previously, came to the missionary and confessed that he had forgotten to set bread for the morning. It was now too late to secure supplies from the village. Moreover, it was impossible to go around to neighbors and gather up sufficient to feed the great crowd the next day.

In simple trust the missionary asked the cook to kneel beside him in the crude little caboose that served as cookhouse for the camp.

Together they placed their problem in God's Hands asking for His help. When they arose at five o'clock in the morning and went out to the caboose—there on the table stood a steaming pile of fresh-baked loaves—sufficient for the day.

The source of supply was never discovered. Yet the event proved a remarkable climax to a wonderful honeymoon, during which some 125 souls came to know Christ!

The Further Refining

FOR THE NEXT FIVE YEARS God in His own gracious, loving, though stern manner, continued to draw this couple to Himself. Again and again they had their confidence in their Heavenly Father tested and refined, for though in the body there were burdens almost too heavy to bear—in the spirit there were seasons of uplift and exaltation. In the hours of trial they learned to place implicit reliance in the all-wise purposes of God. Resting in Him they discovered that the fires of temptation lost their heat and the pain of their problems lost its sting.

It was during this time that the missionary had accepted a pastorate in a city church for a time. His wife was expecting their first child, and the need for suitable nourishing food was most urgent. It was their custom, especially after the long and demanding duties of the Sunday services, to meet quietly in a secluded restaurant for a hearty meal enjoyed in the gentle contentment of the week's work well done.

41

The church treasurer was in the habit of handing them a cheque for $25.00 each Sunday evening. This constituted not only the remuneration for their services, but also the sum upon which they counted for their Sunday evening treat—since each weekend found them living on very slim rations indeed with so meagre an income.

It was very near the time for the child to be born, and as usual Sunday evening had rolled around once more with its $25.00 cheque and the happy prospect of dining out for a change. On this particular evening, following the service, the missionary and his wife were just closing up the church after the folks had gone home, when a grey-haired, elderly lady, greatly agitated, came into the church.

She was in a desperate plight. Her son, who was somewhat of a rebel, had been thrown into gaol, and she needed $25.00 to release him. Could they help her in her distress?

As the missionary and his wife looked at each other knowingly—it was in the knowledge that this evening there would be no meal for them. Instead it would be a dismal tramp back to a one-room apartment where the cupboards stood empty and almost bare.

In spite of this they knew they could not spurn the demand made upon them. The $25.00 cheque was endorsed, turned over to the woman, and she went to her son's relief.

Bleakly the couple walked home—comforting one another in the thought that in their own dire need God would not forsake them.

Perhaps the morning mail or some visitor would bring them succour and relief. Yet no such help came to them in their extremity.

For three days their diet consisted of little hard biscuits fashioned from the scrapings of flour, raisins and salt which was all their food that remained. They would bow over this simple fare asking God to bless it to the strength of bodies desperately in need of much more. These hard pellets were then soaked in water in an attempt to render them more palatable.

Finally the young woman could stand it no longer. She broke

down in tears amid her distress. That same morning, her husband, as was his custom, set out on his rounds to visit his members. In this he was continually urged on by his wife who again and again made the remark: "Take care of God's work! He'll take care of us!"

His first call was at a charwoman's home. She greeted him at the door by putting into his hand a dollar bill. Then she told him of a gorgeous blouse she had purchased for herself at the exorbitant price of $12.00. Surely she had been altogether too extravagant in doing this. Perhaps his wife would like to have it instead. So she pressed it upon him and he left the house in light spirits.

His next call was at a florist establishment owned and operated by one of the deacons in the church.

"Oh!" the proprietor exclaimed on seeing the pastor enter the shop, "I've been intending to send your wife some flowers for a long time. Here, would you take this dozen and a half of American Beauty roses home to her?"

To be sure he would, and thus he left the store, his arms full of flowers, a blouse and the dollar bill burning a hole in his pocket.

Just as he went to board a streetcar, there was a shout to him from a man across the street: "Wait, wait! I've got something for you!" Darting through the traffic he dashed over and thrust an envelope in the missionary's pocket. "It's a cheque for $25.00 that I've been intending to give you all week," he gasped, half out of breath. "Ever since I made it out last Sunday it's been bothering me."

When the missionary arrived back at the bare little one-room apartment, he found his wife down on her knees, scrubbing the floor and weeping.

"Oh," she sobbed," I just wanted to show the Lord how sorry I am that I ever doubted Him."

Tenderly she was picked up from the task which she should never have tackled. In her lap her husband laid the beautiful blouse, the magnificent roses, the cheque for $25.00 and what was now left of the dollar bill.

In mixed floods of joy and relief, a fine dinner was soon prepared—and what a dinner that was! Never was any meal more beautifully garnished with praise to God for His unfailing goodness.

Even more remarkable was the fact that in spite of such privations, their first child was delivered a strong and bouncing babe, again proof of their Heavenly Father's unchanging faithfulness to His children—those whose trust is ever in Him.

In spite of such deepening experiences, the pastoring of the city church was not without its discouraging moments. Especially was this true for the young backwoods missionary who confessed himself woefully short of either sacred or secular training . . . not having had formal theological schooling of any sort.

To make matters more thorny his heterogeneous congregation was composed of older devout people of deep and distinct convictions, whose theoretical knowledge of God's Word far surpassed his own.

At first he attempted to meet the challenge of their censure in his own strength. The result was that not only did the numbers dwindle pitifully, but also an acute distress of mind which he could not shake overtook him.

Finally one night in deep anguish of soul he went out to walk the streets seeking solace for his spirit. From the depths of his heart he cried out, "Oh, God, why don't You let me die? Why don't You cast me out?"

In that moment there came to him a Voice which said: "Receive your sight, your faith has made you whole!"

In an instant he was transported from a state of despondency to one of utter confidence that God would vindicate His Word.

He rushed home, awoke his wife, and shouted happily, "It's going to be all right—everything is going to be all right."

"How—what do you mean?" she asked a little bewildered.

The answer came quickly. From that day he preached Christ to his critical congregation. They could see Christ and only Christ. In Him the members of the congregation became as one. The Spirit of God moved amongst them graciously in mighty power, melting hearts in the warmth of His love.

Shortly after this awakening and refreshment in the church, an invitation came for the missionary to take over the large and imposing church where originally he had been converted.

With divided mind he turned to God seeking only His will. Because there lay ever present that temptation to be drawn by men away from the lonely paths of service to which God had called him, it was necessary to seek God's face.

It is not surprising to find, then, that instead of taking the more attractive offer of a pretentious pastorate with its prestige, he turned his face once more toward the frontier bush country and there plunged back into his pioneer work with the loggers and woodsmen.

Thus there passed some seven years of fitting, refining, and sharpening. Not all those years were glorious with the hot fires of victory. There were dark years too—years in which there were the cool ashes of indifference or at best mere smouldering embers of a once-vital life.

But God does not forsake His own. No matter at what great distance they may walk, His love never flags. Gently and tenderly men are wooed and drawn back into the paths beside still waters of contentment, where once again they delight in intimate comradeship with the great and gentle Shepherd of their souls.

Several more years of working amongst the loggers of Western Washington were all that was needed now to finally equip this couple for the precise lifework God had been preparing them to shoulder. Again they stood at the crossroads in life. This time the invitation was not to forsake their backwoods calling for a large church, as it had been the first time. Rather now the call was to embark on an extensive evangelistic campaign across the United States.

In an agony of indecision, they sought the mind of God. To forsake the plan of God's choice or be deflected from His purpose was now unthinkable. Finally in an attitude of utter submission to God's will and wishes for them, they prayed early one morning before dawn, that that very day, somehow, they should know His purposes. As by a miracle, in the mail that morning there came to them an outright invitation to join the Shantymen's Association of North America, to become their missionary on Vancouver Island. That was the answer they sought. Immediately they accepted and thus in 1930 commenced their ministry with this association that has lasted up to the present hour.

The Power Behind the Scenes

ONE OF THE REMARKABLE MYSTERIES of God's dealing with men is the manner in which individuals are prepared in advance, unbeknown to each other, to become a powerful team working together for the advancement of His cause.

While the Missionary and his wife were in their backwoods environment being chiselled and chopped into shape to fit the niche God had in mind for them on the Island, He was also fashioning others to become powerful companions in this Shantymen's work.

There was on Vancouver Island a sprightly little man of immense energy and wholehearted dedication to God's service. To those who knew and loved him—as most did who ever met him—he was always known as Uncle Sammy.

Here was a man literally full of springs, who appeared to be dancing along with sheer enthusiasm for life. His mind was quick and able to conceive great dreams upon which he found ways of putting solid flesh and bones.

Uncle Sammy had been appointed as the representative and manager of the Cadbury Fry people on Vancouver Island. In his travels, especially throughout the unchurched parts of the Island, he became deeply concerned for the spiritual well-being of the backwoodsmen and rural ranchers.

Unlike most people who never became concerned quite enough to put their concern into action, he promptly decided to do something about it. Moving as he did amongst Christian folk, he soon gathered about him a small group whose primary purpose was to pray for these frontiersmen of the Island. This little handful of people met in a small hall of the Episcopal church in Victoria. It was about 1927 that this prayer group was formed, and a year later Uncle Sammy contacted the Shantymen's Association to see what might be done to procure a missionary for Vancouver Island.

This small beginning had its precarious moments. The interest of the participants flagged—their numbers dwindled and the outlook was bleak. People always seem to want to back a winning team, and few have enough of the Mind of God to realize that in His estimation very small things and weak things can be of momentous consequence. The upshot was that eventually one noon hour, which was the customary time for this group to meet—dear old Uncle Sammy found himself standing alone in the room without a single praying companion. No one had come. He felt utterly deserted. No doubt a little like Elijah at the low point of his career. However God sometimes has to get men absolutely alone before He can show Himself real to them.

That noon hour in a sense of total abandonment to the purpose of God—whatever it might be—Uncle Sammy stood alone in that empty mocking room and cried out, "Oh, God—if this is your work—send someone today to let me know if you wish me to carry on!"

While engaged in prayer he thought he detected a slight scratching sound at the door. Immediately he looked up and with his quick movements stepped over to the door, finding that an envelope had been thrust under it. He tore it open and read this note: "I'm so sorry I could not attend today, but enclosed is ten dollars for you to carry on this work."

From that day there was not a shadow of doubt in Uncle Sammy's mind as to the authority of this work to which he was called. Nothing could deflect him from it—nothing could turn him to the right hand or to the left.

This prayer group continued to meet regularly for prayer

each week at the noon hour over a period of some three years without having any active missionary in the field.

Then there was found a fine elderly Scotsman who took it upon himself to visit the scattered stump ranches and backwoods farmers scattered over the Island. His spirit was shining and bright; but he was weak in body and almost blind. This work soon proved to be far beyond his strength.

So it was that just at this crucial juncture, one of the members of the prayer group, who had been well-acquainted with the work of the young backwoods missionary in Alberta and Washington, suggested to the committee of the group that they should invite him to join them as their Shantymen missionary on the Island . . . which of course he did on that wonderful morning that their letter arrived in answer to prayer for guidance.

From these shaky beginnings the number of participants in this prayer group and their faithfulness to the Shantymen's cause has increased and gained great strength. It is perhaps not overstating the simple facts in the case to declare that this body of devoted, dedicated, praying people has been the essential power behind the scenes which for the past thirty years has made the Shantymen's ministry so blessed to so many.

These men and women—most of them elderly—many of only meagre means—coming from all strata of society and every branch of Christendom—have in common a desire to see God's work progress on the Island . . . and pray to that one end. *No wonder it does.*

If throughout the chapters which follow you are amazed at the remarkable manner in which God provides for the work of the Shantymen—remember that these sincere humble people are behind the scenes praying for the provision of those needs necessary to the work.

If you are astounded at God's protection over these hardy missionaries, who time and again are exposed to the unchained fury of the Pacific in their small craft—remind yourself that there is a powerful group praying back in Victoria for their safety while at sea.

If you are overwhelmed by God's power to transform the lives of men and women who have literally struck rock bottom on the skid roads of life; who are lifted up to become citizens of honour to themselves and to God—it is because an unsung band of dedicated men and women meet regularly for prayer to move the Hand of God on others' behalf.

To attend one of these prayer groups is in itself an exhilarating experience for any newcomer. Their obvious enthusiasm, their contagious delight in their common cause, their spontaneous interest and support of even the smallest venture of faith make for a heartwarming adventure in the realm of simple, yet powerful Christian living.

After coming away from such a gathering there inevitably leaps to mind those famous lines by Lord Alfred Tennyson:

> More things are wrought by prayer than this [old] world dreams of.

With Pack and Paddle

WHEN THE MISSIONARY joined the Shantymen work on Vancouver Island it was in very truth a case of "coming home." The Island had been the scene of his birth and boyhood so that immediately he felt at ease in surroundings which were most natural and familiar to him.

More important, however, was the fact that now, for the first time since his commitment to God ten years before, he was absolutely assured that the command given to him then was being carried out in his Christian career. For the initial verse implanted in his heart at his conversion was Mark 5:19: "Go home to thy friends, and tell them how great things the Lord hath done for thee, and hath had compassion on thee."

This was indeed the very thing that was being done now, and for the next thirty years or more of his subsequent ministry this assurance continued to be a source of great delight and contentment to him in his work for the cause of Jesus Christ his Lord and Master.

The first days on the coast were both lone and hard. To fully understand the difficulties of travel over this field it is important to remember that there were no roads on the West Coast thirty years ago. The task of punching highways through the rock

51

ridges and tremendous timber of the region was something not envisaged until the advent of caterpillar bulldozers and massive earth-moving machinery of later years.

Because of this there were only tiny trails, most of them short tortuous paths that wound their way inland short distances from coastal points. There were no main lateral routes apart from linesmen's trails which were emergency measures whereby lightkeepers and shipwrecked seamen could make contact with the outside world. So the only way to reach folks on the coast was either to hit the trails on foot with a pack on back or else to travel by small boat from point to point. Hiking on coastal trails can be anything but a picnic. The heavy rains, the dark brooding skies, the gloom of heavy dank growth crowding the path, the ever present timber standing tall and silent beside the way—all of this wrapped in mist and moisture, requiring heavy rainproof clothing—make walking heavy and the miles dismally long.

It is not hard to understand, then, why it soon became apparent that boat travel was not only a much more practical but also a more efficient way in which to reach the isolated families who had strung themselves like beads upon the silver strand of water that encircled the Island.

In 1932 the Missionary decided to establish his base at Ucluelet, situated on the Northwest flank of Barkley Sound. There he hired an Indian seal-hunting canoe, a craft seventeen feet long, with two sets of oars. It was sturdily constructed to stand heavy seas with an outturned gunwhale that prevented the craft from taking too much water in a rough slop.

The summer's first major expedition in this canoe was made with a young lad of eighteen from Sooke as a rowing companion, each man handling a pair of oars. To accompany them through the maze of treacherous channels, reefs and tidal waters of the West Coast, a young Indian Christian was taken along as a guide. He directed the craft over the dangerous reefs and helped by paddling at the stern.

The trip was a thoroughly wet, sodden safari, during which the three men were soaked most of the time. The only relief

Part of the "Power Behind the Scenes"

Shantymen

Part of the "Power on the Job"

Shantymen

W. Phillip Keller

"Just Sitting" Is Sometimes the Surest Path to Another's Heart

The Young Missionary Welds a Firm Friendship

Life

came at night. They would beach the canoe, stretch a small tarpaulin over themselves, and in its shelter build a wet-wood fire on which to cook their meagre fare.

In this way they visited from house to house, village to village, bay to bay, laying the sturdy groundwork of man-to-man friendship which would inevitably prove to be the foundation for all their future work.

One such visit was to a treacherous little cove known as Useless Inlet. It had probably earned this name because its mouth was blocked by a treacherous reef of rock which made it impossible for any ship to enter the passage except at very high tides.

On a grey rainy evening the missionary canoe worked her way into this inlet and grated onto the gravel beach inside. There on the soaking shore the tarp was stretched, a heaping fire was built and in the twilight the men decided to invite the residents of the bay to an informal service.

Only four old bachelors made their homes in this dismal spot. Each in his own right was a colourful character whose house was either a mere rotting shack on the beach or an ancient boat pulled up above the tide line. One of these used a four-gallon gas can as his stove, with pieces of rusty tin for stovepipes sticking through the leaking roof of his boat—whose only dry spot was the forecastle where he whiled away the drab winter days.

A second passed under the colourful name of Hi-Jack Davis whose chief pastime seemed to be the concoction of weird and wonderful yarns about his beloved West Coast. He told of fashioning himself a powerful slingshot with which to hunt the monster mosquitoes that haunted Useless Inlet. On his first evening's hunt he fired at one and managed to break its leg, a second escaped him with one eye knocked out, while the third got away with only some missing teeth!

Hi-Jack Davis declared that up until that time he had never minded living in Useless Inlet, but when he awoke the next morning and looked out his window to see three mosquitoes approaching his shack, one on crutches, a second with a glass eye, and the third wearing false teeth, he felt it was just about time to leave.

The third individual known as Gerry the Greek, made a business of gathering small native oysters found in the bay. These were a prize delicacy in those days before the importation of Japanese oysters which have now seeded themselves along the entire coast. Gerry would gather these shellfish, then load them in his antiquated steel-hulled craft with the noble name of "The Iron Duke" and haul them to Kildonan for transport to the outside world. Why the leaky, wheezy boat never went to the bottom a dozen times remains a maritime mystery.

It was with four men of this rough cast gathered about the blazing bonfire that a simple service was held with the eternal rain pelting softly on the canvas overhead—dimpling the water at the shore and dripping off the trees.

A few of the favorite old hymns were sung from a single hymnbook—a passage of Scripture was read—then the grand Good News from God to man told in homespun fashion.

In such a setting the Presence of God Himself was very real and very evident—as evident as though they stood in a cloistered cathedral with a bishop in attendance. Yet none of the men were attired in anything but rough woodsmen's clothes, without ties, white shirts or finery of any sort. Two months' beard was upon their faces and it is doubtful if some of the old bachelors had washed at all that day.

In this sort of setting, and in these humble hearts, God's Word was planted, until not only did many come to believe upon Christ for their salvation, but in Him they found succour, strength and comfort to sustain them in their dreary days on this wilderness frontier.

It is little wonder that the Missionary's young companion returned home to his village in Sooke, fired with enthusiasm for the West Coast work. When at the end of the season the Missionary returned to Victoria to report on the summer's expedition, it was to find several churches already eager to welcome him to tell of the Shantymen's endeavours. Amongst these was the little church in Sooke where his friend attended.

Here two very significant events took place. Both were to have far-reaching consequences in the days ahead. There were in the audience that evening an important businessman in the community—the head of the Sooke Harbour Fishing Company— and a small ten-year-old lad who happened to be visiting in the village at the time.

After the service the businessman approached the speaker and asked him if he intended to make further trips by canoe up the coast. When assured that he certainly did—the businessman ejaculated, "Indeed you're not going to hire a canoe again! I have a whole fleet of fine fishing boats tied up down there at the dock! Come down and take your pick!"

This was done in due course and the boat chosen for their next major cruise was a beautiful fifty-foot fishboat named the "Otter Point."

With a full complement of eight persons on board, including a retired doctor from the China Inland Mission, this boat was to be greatly blessed and widely used to great advantage the following summer.

A no-less-spectacular transaction had taken place, however, in the heart of a ten-year-old boy in that same service. Moved by the message, and the obvious need for the Shantymen to have a proper boat in their work, he decided to do more than just talk about it.

That night he went back to the house where he was staying, deep in thought. God was working in his heart. He climbed down into the basement of the old house and dug out a large-mouthed quart sealer with a metal top. This he quietly took up to his room and punched a hole through the lid with his jackknife. Through this hole he dropped all of his money—precisely two pennies. Then down in the kitchen he found a scrap of paper on which he scrawled in his crude boyish handwriting —"For a Shantyman Boat." This he took and stuck to the bottle. Humbly he asked God to bless this little sum allowing it to grow into a worthwhile fund for the Shantymen. Then without disclosing his secret, he hid the jar quietly in a corner of his closet.

If ever there was a practical demonstration of a person not

letting his left hand know what his right hand did, this was it. For God who saw in secret was soon to reward him openly.

A few days later the good lady of the house in cleaning the boy's room, quite by accident came across the jar with its pennies. When she read the label, the impact of its meaning struck straight to the depths of her own heart. Deeply moved in mind by this bold and selfless act she immediately spread the news around as only a woman can. Her husband hearing of it was the first to take what money he could spare and add it to the jar. The incident captured the public imagination of Christians far and near who heard of it. In very short order, during those moneyless, hungry thirties, money began to come in from all directions from young and old, until the jar was so stuffed with cash it could not contain another penny.

Some three months later the Missionary was invited back to speak at the same community hall in Sooke. At the close of his service he was presented with the jar full to overflowing with money, by a group of young people with radiant hearts. Here was the very keel—the first timber—in a fund which grew and grew into the full and final building of a boat designed and equipped specifically for the West Coast.

God's ways are not our ways, nor our methods His methods. . . . Just as a few small loaves and fishes once fed so many—so two copper pennies, given unreservedly to Him, were to produce dividends beyond any man's ability to measure in eternal values.

The "Otter Point"

IN SEVERAL RESPECTS the initial cruise made in the "Otter Point" was amongst the most important ever made by the Shantymen on the West Coast. First of all it enabled them to visit virtually every bay and inlet from Victoria to Kyuquot Sound, thus covering a tremendous territory in one summer. This would otherwise have been quite impossible in so short a time by the more laborious means of a canoe.

Secondly this sweeping survey revealed at a single stroke the appalling conditions under which many of the West Coast folk were living during the dreadful depression. On every hand poverty stalked naked and unashamed; not only poverty of purse but also of medical help and spiritual succour.

It is true that here and there a lone missionary of the older established churches stood rooted to some savage spot, trying earnestly to maintain a witness for a pitiful handful of parishioners in the face of ruthless odds. On the other hand there was no mobile marine work that could move rapidly from place to place as a need presented itself; nor was there any sort of proper, consistent medical service for a population that numbered in the thousands.

To the Shantymen, some of whose committee were on board during this trip, it became abundantly clear that here was an immense field on their back doorstep. It was an area into which they would have to sink their roots very deep to weather its hardships, and which would require sturdy men and sturdy boats to face its dangers.

The "Otter Point" which had been loaned by the Sooke Harbour Fishing Company, was a seine boat, a trim fifty-foot craft of fine lines and sturdy construction. She operated on a three-cylinder Union Gas engine that literally gobbled up the gas in fearsome quantities as she plowed through the water up and down the coast.

Besides the Missionary and his son, there were on board five members of the Shantymen's Committee; a doctor recently retired from service in China; and the same Indian who had been guide on the first canoe trips.

Provisioning this boat was in itself a major enterprise. Still, even in this, God's Hand was most apparent. The manner in which a very substantial store of medical supplies was laid in was itself remarkable. The doctor had made a complete list of dispensary items he felt would be necessary for the summer.

This was submitted to a wholesale druggist, with instructions that the goods be sent down to the ship C.O.D. since at the time the order was placed funds were not available to pay for it.

When the Missionary saw the delivery truck approaching the ship, coming down the wharf, with this large and expensive consignment, his heart began to fail him, for there was still no money on hand to pay the bill. He almost felt inclined to flee, hoping that somehow the goods might be left, to be paid for later.

Just at this crucial moment as the delivery truck approached from one side, a well-dressed gentleman walked up to the boat from the other side and introduced himself.

"A friend asked me to bring you this gift today," he remarked casually, handing the Missionary a sealed envelope.

When a few moments later the C.O.D. bill was presented by the truck driver, to their unbounded joy the Missionary and his companions, on opening the envelope from the stranger, discovered that it contained a sum of money exactly sufficient to meet the account.

This was accepted as a very special token of approval from God's Hand upon their outset of the journey.

In the supply of food, clothing and those supplies essential to a successful cruise God was most gracious in laying these requirements upon the hearts of friends. They shared of their meagre incomes or home-grown products to stock the "Otter Point" to capacity.

The ship's company were busy indeed as they slowly made their way up the coast. The doctor alone treated 273 cases, several of which were minor operations of various degrees. A great deal of dentistry was done while hampers of used clothing were distributed amongst the most needful and poverty-stricken families.

Wherever it was possible to hold meetings and conduct services, whether at fish canneries or in logging camps, this was done. The response to such efforts was heartwarming beyond their wildest dreams, for many of those frontiersmen had not enjoyed any worship for months, so that their hunger for spiritual refreshment was keen and compelling.

As week followed week of such endeavours the great unsatisfied need of the West Coast became an ever more constraining burden upon the hearts of the men. Somehow, in some way they must meet the challenge.

One intriguing incident that occurred about this time related to the rather monotonous diet of canned food and fish of the men on board. Fresh meat was virtually unobtainable, yet a formidable craving for beef of some sort gnawed at their vitals.

Finally the Missionary suggested that since this was something beyond his ability to produce from the bleak coast of stunted trees and raging seas, perhaps they should pray about it. This they did—asking that if it pleased God, somehow a feed of fresh meat should be procured.

That night after holding a service in the fish camp at Cee-peecee, a big rough Scandinavian who cooked for the camp approached the Missionary and said: "I would just be so glad to give you something for your work, but I have no money. Would you accept a roast of fresh beef instead?"

The reply was not slow in coming. Immediately he led the men back into the giant cooler of his kitchen. There he picked up a massive butcher knife and carved off from one of the sides of beef a choice twelve-pound roast of meat for the fellows.

One can well imagine their happy hearts and the mouth-watering aroma that filled the galley and quarters of the "Otter Point" that night.

Perhaps the most poignant event of this entire summer cruise along the coast took place near Centre Island which lies at the mouth of Esperanza Inlet. Here the ship dropped anchor in a small bight of land. Nearby on the Main Nootka Island there was a tiny bay in the shore where a family from England had been living for more than twenty years.

As the Shantymen approached the land, a man put out from the beach in his canoe to meet them. Getting to within hailing distance, he called out to them: "Are you fish buyers?"

The call came back: "No, we're missionaries."

Without waiting another moment the man back-paddled his canoe and sped for the shore not lingering to talk at all.

When the eight men from the "Otter Point" landed on the beach they were welcomed by two men and two women weeping unashamedly.

They pressed themselves on the missionaries, invited them into their simple little cottage and bade them sit down to tea. Then they shared the best they had of their frugal fare with the men.

Bit by bit their story unfolded with all the simplicity and drama that is part of the pageantry of West Coast life.

For more than twenty years this family had eked out a

meagre existence on this bleak gale-lashed shore. Their mail came once every ten days, and just the day before, newspapers had reached them telling of steps being taken by the large churches on the mainland to extend missionary work up the main coast and along the inside passage of Vancouver Island.

"But not a single mention was made of sending a missionary out here to the lonely West Coast where we have waited for so long."

With sobbing broken voices they went on: "And so a great bitterness filled our hearts . . . a bitterness that those who already could get to churches should be given even more encouragement—while we who never have had anything should be forgotten!"

Their claim was more than true. But they continued: "Still we could not let the bitterness remain. Instead we got down on our knees last night and prayed earnestly that God would send us some missionaries. And here you are today!"

Their joy in the faithfulness of God was unbounded. No wonder the Shantymen were so deeply stirred. Then their hosts recounted how their elderly father had been taken ill in this place. Because the nearest doctor was more than one hundred miles away over angry water, no medical assistance could be provided for him. In their simple, rough, rude manner they nursed him as best they could until his death.

With heavy hearts they hunted the beaches for driftwood planks and boards with which to build a coffin. In this crude box they carried him to a height of land, just below a high rock where he loved to sit and scan the ocean during his lifetime. There in the wild stony ground they dug a grave, and buried his remains, planting a rustic wooden cross at the head.

"We took a Bible and did our best to give him a fitting service," they cried out between sobs, "but oh, what we would have given to have a missionary here."

Standing on that rocky promontory, overlooking the surging seas, with the pioneer grave beside them, there came to the Shantymen more clearly than ever before the challenging call of service to this rugged coast.

Building "Messenger II"

I N SPITE OF the obvious and burning need of a boat work on the West Coast that had become so very clear during the "Otter Point" cruise, not all of the Shantymen's committee were unanimously agreed that this was the work for them to undertake.

After all, the traditions of the Shantymen's Association were deeply entrenched in the concept of their missionaries tramping backwoods trails on foot—pack on back—very much a part of solid soil. One of those who clung most tenaciously to this idea was the treasurer himself.

It was in his care that the contents of the small lad's jar had been placed—which together with other donations had now accumulated to a three-hundred-dollar boat fund.

It transpired, however, in the providence of God that this same gentleman made a trip to the mainland, and while there happened to visit in the home of an enthusiastic young Christian boat builder in the city of New Westminster. This craftsman was not only of a most untiring spirit himself but also passionately fond of small boats. Over a period of time he had become head of a boatbuilding firm in that city.

It was his enthusiasm for the plan of using small boats in mission work, coupled with an offer to undertake the building of a sturdy craft especially suited to West Coast conditions, that turned the trend of thought in the treasurer's mind. The latter now returned to Victoria very much enthused with the offer and naturally found full support for this new venture of faith.

The Missionary, who of course had spearheaded the project from its earliest point, requested permission to take the three-hundred-dollar boat fund, proceed to New Westminster, and commence work immediately on the boat. This was agreed to, though no one at the time had any notion how many thousands of dollars would eventually be required for the building.

Depositing the $300.00 in the bank in New Westminster, the Missionary and his companion builder threw themselves whole-heartedly into the work. The craftsman gave unstintingly of his time and skill. Often at the end of the day their hands would be bruised and bleeding from shaping steaming oak ribs and tough fir planking that went into the hull. But this was a labour of love.

Week upon week—plank upon plank—bolt upon bolt, the very finest of materials went into her construction. No pains were spared to turn out the most seaworthy craft possible.

During all this time not a single appeal was made for funds to anyone. But the enthusiasm of the men working on the hull was a contagion that spread from person to person until it became common knowledge that a mission boat was on the way. Men and women, boys and girls from all over the lower mainland came to look, watch, and return home moved enough to act on their impulses.

The upshot was that money continued to come in, sufficient to meet every bill that was presented. No expense was spared to put the finest of lumber and metal into a hull destined to endure tremendous batterings on some of the world's worst water.

Finally the day for launching had arrived. Yet marvel of marvels there still remained in the bank account $400.00—more than had been in the boat fund initially.

That evening the Missionary rambled around the neighborhood in his old Model T Ford gathering up all the youngsters who had watched the growth of the boat from keel to wheel-house with such fascination.

They were turned loose to explore the ship from top to bottom.

Gay laughter and excited cries rang through her timbers and filled her quarters. What a send-off she had!

Amid all this gaiety and hilarious excitement, one tiny five-year-old girl slipped up beside the Missionary and tucked her tiny hand in his rough strong palm so calloused from handling tools and timber. "Daddy," she said, looking up into his strong brown face, "I'm going to pray that God will give you the bedding for the boat."

This was the spontaneous, unprompted impulse of a small child's simple trust.

The next day the Missionary was back in the city of Victoria, addressing a supper meeting sponsored by that faithful band of praying people who meet each week in the Y.W.C.A. There he told of the amazing manner in which the Lord had provided for their expenses at each stage of construction, through the kindness of interested friends.

In his audience was a stranger lady, who a few moments before had been passing by on the street and was invited to come in for the service. Much to the amusement of the Missionary this woman, who sat in the very front row, persisted in knitting steadily all through his address. She was obviously quite impressed by what she heard, for at the close she hurriedly jumped to her feet and addressed the people: "I hope you will not feel I am out of order. But I came all the way to Victoria from Montreal for the single purpose of playing winter golf here. This story of the 'Messenger II' has made such an impact on me, that I feel we people of Montreal should have a part in the boat. If your treasurer would permit me now, I would like to give him a cheque for $25.00. May I say I would like it to go for bedding on board!"

This last sentence was like a thunderclap in the Missionary's mind, because he had made no mention whatever of his small daughter's desire to the audience. In such gentle ways, and by such tender faith does God see fit to fulfill His trustworthiness to mankind—very young children included.

"Messenger II" was now towed to Victoria, down the Fraser River, across the Straits of Georgia, into her home port. Here the engine was to be installed and the final outfitting completed that would equip her for the rugged days ahead.

The Shantymen were offered a used motor which could be installed and paid for with the $400.00 remaining in the bank account. It was felt, however, that because of the treacherous seas she was to sail—oftentimes bearing strangers and friends whose lives would depend on her—it was only right that a new power plant be installed. This would of course cost much more and funds were short.

It was decided to call a day of prayer, to seek God's will and guidance in the decision. Those who took part were told that this was not a ruse to raise money, since no donations made that day would be accepted, nor would a plea for help be made. It was Thursday that the day was so spent. On Sunday afternoon a government official telephoned the Missionary and requested that he and Uncle Sammy come to his house together. This they did in wonderment. At the house they were given a letter which came from an anonymous donor. A binding condition was attached to the envelope that they could claim its contents only if they agreed never to try and discover who had sent it.

To this they agreed, then opened the letter with utter amazement and astonishment. Out of it fell a sheaf of hundred-dollar notes, more than ample to not only install a brand-new engine in "Messenger II" but also to entirely equip and complete her furnishings. In addition there was money to stock all the food lockers, fill the tanks with gasoline, and supply the necessary lubricants for her operation!

God's faithfulness to those prepared to rest in His unfailing goodness surpasses men's greatest expectations. It is never God who betrays us, rather it is we who have not the faith equivalent to one grain of sand in Pachena Bay.

To recount the full story of the thirteen years that this tough little boat brought strength, courage, and comfort to the isolated men and women of the Island would in itself pack a book with drama. Two examples will illustrate this point.

Once she came around Estevan Point with a tremendous stern sea making up from the West. Already she had endured a serious pounding from the twenty-five-foot combers that struck her abeam as she came down the coast. So ferocious were the winds and water this day, as she headed into Refuge Cove (now called Hot Springs Cove), that the sea had been literally beaten to a froth. The foam and spume for a mile out to sea was so deep that only the deck and wheelhouse were visible above it. The entire hull was completely buried from sight in the foam as she felt her way cautiously through the narrow channel into sheltered waters.

On another occasion she had a narrow escape while running down from Quatsino Sound toward Kyuquot Sound. As she approached Cape Cook with its notorious rough seas a strong wind was making up on the outside, churning the water into raging whitecaps.

It was decided to take shelter in Klaskish. This tiny hole-in-the-wall is sometimes referred to as one of the windiest spots in the world.

The tiny haven lies at the foot of a series of mountains which encircle the cove. The wind strikes these heights, ricochets off them and spirals down with plunging fury into the bay itself. So tremendous can this downdraft be, that small boats have actually been blown under water here.

"Messenger II" entered this harbour with misgiving—not knowing what to expect. There were no other boats there, so the anchor was dropped and there she lay calm and safe through the night. The next morning at dawn she put out to sea again because the storm had abated. There she was met by the Police Patrol boat, who having seen her head south the day before, out of Quatsino Sound, felt sure she had foundered in the blow. Through such adversities, and many more, God's Hand of protection was upon the tiny craft as it plied up and down this wild, wind-battered strand which was its mission field.

Coast Characters

I T CAN BE readily appreciated by anyone who understands
human nature, that a country with the rugged and tumultuous geographical topography of the Pacific Coast, is bound to
have characters of matching temper.

Those rough, tough individuals who choose this untamed
strand as a homeland, must have steel in their spirits and brim-
stone in their blood to withstand its violence and its depression.

To merely attempt a general word description of such folk
would be tiresome. We can, therefore, do no better than recount some of the instances in which God in His great mercy
took hold of rebellious men and women, transforming them
into citizens of credit not only to their country, but also to His
Kingdom.

Above all it is most necessary to remind ourselves that such
results arise from the persistent, undaunted, dogged determination of missionaries, doctors, nurses and Christian women audacious enough, on God's behalf, to keep going back to their
folk again and again. It is akin to the persistent pounding of
waves on granite until it crumbles under their impact.

Some of these backwoods people have been visited over and
over, without any visible sign of change in their characters. Then
one day under the impact of God's Word, or perchance by a

stray remark guided by God's Spirit, a crack will suddenly appear in the hard crusty character—and through it light will flood a life, which up till then was dark and despicable.

God's pardon is overwhelmingly generous—it is still extended to all men and women, of every color, every creed and every character.

Nor has its power to alter mankind waned one whit since Christ Himself pardoned the thief who hung beside Him on the Cross.

OLAF THE LOGGER

Olaf was of Viking stock. He was a man amongst men, who like most of his bachelor comrades of the bush, lived for payday and the big "blow out" on the town. In a single weekend he would squander his entire month's earnings, by going on a terrific bender at the "Goat Ranch," a synonym for the nearest beer parlour.

Olaf's life was either all play—with wine, women, and song—or all work as he filled out his long drab weeks in the logging camp. He lived life to its dregs, and knew what sin was all about, as steadily he went on destroying himself. On Olaf's bunk, as on every other bed in the bunkhouse, the Missionary left a booklet with some Scripture portions. Slowly and laboriously the logger began to read this literature, for he was not highly educated. The contents seeped gently into his mind, and he became troubled in spirit.

The next time the Missionary called, the foreman asked him if he would talk to Olaf. "I think he's going crazy," he remarked, as he sent for the lanky logger.

Gently the Missionary dealt with the man, trying earnestly to have him open up. For a long time he was adamant—then the crack came and it was obvious he was under deep conviction.

There and then he was presented with the call of Christ upon his life. He yielded himself to God and shouted enthusiastically, "It feels like 15,000 tons rolled off my back!"

Biting into Big Timber

Bucking a "Stick" on the Beach

Topping a Spar Tree   *Government of B.C., Canada*

Loading Logs

Government of B.C., Canada

Three months later the Missionary came again. Olaf was living in the Word. He pored over the Book till late at night, reading by candles or oil lamp. He read the Bible so avidly others thought he was mad. Where before all his thoughts were of drink, demoiselles, and dancing—now Christ was the center of his affections. Tenderly he spoke to others of his Saviour—even remonstrating with the boss for using God's name in profanity. His face now shone with the Glory of God, and when years later the Missionary was called to his funeral, it was in the knowledge that here was one of God's colourful saints gone Home.

THE VETERAN

He had been savagely wounded in the first war. A bursting shell scarred his face deeply. A fragment tore away the nose bridge from his face. Now he could neither smell nor scarcely taste his food. His damaged eyes were blinded beyond hope. The same shell had injured his backbone and shattered a knee.

Thus he sat, hour upon dreadful hour, month upon dragged-out month, in a darkened room, the blinds drawn, submerging and stupefying his stunted senses in tobacco and drink. He was a shattered hulk of human flesh. Within that hulk smouldered an unquenchable spirit of venom and bitter hatred against man, God, and life itself.

One day the Missionary knocked at the door of his cottage, that stood back in the trees, a little ways from the winding valley road.

When told that there was a missionary at the door, he shouted vehemently to his wife: "A missionary—show him in!"

She, knowing what would happen, had already shut the door in the Missionary's face, telling him to be gone.

But at the veteran's insistence, he entered the dark room, where the wreck of a man sat betwixt his cases of ale and humidor of tobacco and pipes. The veteran launched into a terrible tirade against God, the church, Christ, and missionaries.

So violent and vindictive was the abuse heaped on him that the Missionary could not answer a word. His heart ached and wept for the man—and in anguish of spirit he sought guidance from God. Quietly he opened to Psalm 51 and there began to read: "Purge me with hyssop, and I shall be clean. Wash me, and I shall be whiter than snow. Make me to hear joy and gladness, that the bones which Thou hast broken may rejoice."

In an instant of time the man was brokenhearted. The rebellion was gone—and he bowed penitently before Almighty God.

In that hour he responded to the loving tender Voice of the Saviour saying: "Come unto me, all ye that labour and are heavy laden, and I will give you rest."

It was a few months later that a letter reached the Missionary from this man. In it he was enthusiastic about God and what a change had been performed in his heart. It concluded with this sentence: "Today for the first time in all these years I smelled the roses in my garden. I saw too in a new way all the beauty with which God surrounds me!"

What a transformation. Do some of us still doubt that God lives? Do we doubt that He is *concerned* about *us?*

THE WEARY WOMAN

The West Coast is a harsh drab place for men. It is much more so for women. At least the men can get out of the house, and in an atmosphere of daring adventure carry on their dangerous jobs of logging, fishing, mining, or land clearing.

For the women there is no such release from the eternal confinement of four walls. There is no escape from the grey skies, the dripping trees, the grey sea, the misty mountains. For a woman a home can become a grey-walled prison in winter. Add to this the burden of never-ending stacks of soiled dishes; the endless track of muddy boots in the door; the inevitable youngsters straining at the leash to go out into the muck, and if not allowed to, getting in each other's hair with flying fists and frayed tempers. Top this off with the lonely isolation; the chilling, clinging dampness of the fog and rain; the wet clothes hanging sodden from the ceiling filling the house with their rank, steamy smell. This is a woman's winter world on the coast.

Little wonder so many of these women turn to liquor to escape from their enviroment. No other place on the continent has as high a rate of alcoholism. Little marvel too that often amongst the women and children the Missionary found his greatest field of service.

This particular lady, however, had more than just these problems to confront her. Actually, being the wife of a mill boss, she enjoyed a better-than-average home besides all the amenities which her husband's substantial salary could provide.

Her major burden was her two boys who fought like indomitable wildcats. In fact so violent was their dislike for each other that just to be in one another's presence meant a scrap.

They would hammer and pound each other until exhausted—even if company was in the house or they were in a strange home.

Their mother had been one of those modern mothers who no doubt used advanced psychological methods of progressive education to rear her boys.

Now they were regular demons who had passed the point of no return.

Fortunately the grandmother was a godly old lady, who prayed fervently that a miracle might happen.

The Missionary chanced to call at the home one day and found the mother utterly distracted. Bursting into tears she cried out: "Oh, what can I do for those boys!" To this the Missionary replied: "You can no longer do anything—but you can cast your burden on the Lord—He careth for you!"

Together they went into the boys' room and kneeled by their beds. There the mother committed herself and her boys to God's care as though she herself were a small child.

The Missionary put his hands upon each of the pillows and prayed that God Almightly would come upon the boys to change and transform their lives.

The next time he dropped around to that home he was met by a beaming and radiant woman. "You should see what God has done," she exclaimed. "Those boys have been changed and the difference is unbelievable, they are just like angels now." So once again, God proved Himself powerful and sufficient for those who entrusted themselves to Him.

THE TEACHER

This single lady was one of those colourful frontier types, who was sturdy in body with a zealous spirit. She was dedicated both to her duty as teacher on the Indian reservation, and also to her Lord and Master.

Being a single white woman, her life on the reservation was not the easiest, although it had proved very rewarding in winning the favor and goodwill of the natives.

Usually though, such tranquil settings are short-lived on "The Graveyard of the Pacific." It was not long until a company of bootleggers decided this was a fruitful field they could not afford to pass up. So they marched right into the reservation the better to sell their brew.

With fiery courage the single lady drove the bootleggers out of the reservation and back to their boats. This did not deter them, for they anchored just offshore and plied a brisk trade with the Indians who came to them in their canoes.

Feelings were now running very high. Intoxicated Indians are difficult to deal with at the best of times. A band of them came to the teacher threatening to invade her meeting that night and wreck the premises. In fact they would in turn drive her off the reserve and molest her if she persisted in her teaching.

On this very day the Missionary arrived with his boat. At once she poured out her heart with bitter tears scalding her cheeks: "This—after all my efforts!"

"We will go ahead with a meeting anyway tonight," was his reply. Into the hall, lighted with its flickering oil lamps, the Indians crowded that night—in a manner in which only Indians can compress themselves. The dark faces were tense, set, expectant, eager to see what would explode in this electrified atmosphere.

Across the back of the hall eighteen tough young stalwarts filed in and formed a solid line with their faces hard as flint.

Now there was no escape. The chips were down. The Missionary started in to sing a few verses from the old favorite hymns. It was heavy going at first, but gradually more and more voices joined in the tunes. More hymns were played and sung. They began to have a soothing effect on the crowd. The tensions abated and a gentle atmosphere settled over the little hall.

They kept singing and as the prejudice melted, and hearts softened, a glow began to grow on some of the faces. It was possible to sense the Presence of God's Spirit working in minds and hearts.

Gradually there was a melting and moving in the crowd and to their utter astonishment the eighteen young men came forward and bowed their heads in total penitence before God.

Oh what a transformation! Instead of a brawl, there were men of contrite hearts seeking a Saviour. Such is God's power to change lives.

THE TWO FISHERMEN

At another village, there had been a remarkable number of people who got right with God. In fact some sixty professed to become Christians.

There were here, however, two young fishermen who had continually fought against the Word of God.

To show their defiance, they would go on drinking sprees that lasted days. They would gamble on and on into the night. They would berate those who had taken a Christian stand.

Their money for liquor and gambling finally ran out, so they decided to take their old dilapidated boat with its cantankerous motor, and go fishing, to earn more money for their booze.

At first they had fair success and caught a few salmon. Not satisfied, they pushed out to sea in search of more fish. Then their engine stalled. The two men worked and worked attempting to restart the motor but it would not go. As they lay off shore, wallowing in the waves, a severe storm began to blow up.

Again and again they wrestled with the cantankerous engine

but it simply refused to fire or start. Waves and spray started to blow in and over the cabin, soaking the batteries and motor with brine and salt water. The storm grew and mounted in its fury, blowing them farther and farther out into the broad Pacific, clear out of sight of land.

They were totally exhausted now and lay down in the bottom of the boat as it was driven ruthlessly towards the West. There was nothing they could do to survive. They had no skiff—their meagre supply of food was soon eaten—and they had no fresh water to drink. Thirst became a special agony and torture, because of the alcohol in their blood. Two men adrift on the wide, wide Pacific, lost in the teeth of a storm.

It was in this plight of mind and body that together they fell on their knees and cried out to Almighty God for forgiveness and deliverance. God had allowed them to reach their extremity, that they might seek His face. There on the open sea they confessed their sins to God, making humble repentance for their conduct.

After this, almost in an attitude of utter helplessness they tried starting the motor again. It fired on the first try and ran haltingly. The boat limped slowly back through the wild sea towards land, arriving at a village far to the southeast of where they had set out.

A crowd rushed down to the dock to greet the lost men. There, before a hushed audience of Indians, police and white folk, they recounted their experience in every detail—not omitting to make a bold profession that God had been faithful in preserving them in the face of absolute disaster.

The Stranger's Rest

A NOTHER ENDEAVOUR which roughly paralleled, in time, the development of the early boat work, was the "Stranger's Rest" at Port Alberni.

This refuge for hungry, destitute, unemployed men, who like flotsam, found themselves washed up on the West Coast, was conceived early in the mind of the Missionary. God had endowed this individual with a sincere sympathy for men and women of every walk in life who might be in need of help whether material or spiritual.

To him it was apparent that as the "hungry thirties" gnashed their teeth ever more viciously upon the people of the prairies, the West Coast would in the end feel their fury too. It was only natural that those who could find no work across Canada's wide sprawling wheat plains, would, when winter threatened, drift to the softer climate of the coast.

79

This steady stream of derelict, desperate men grew to flood proportions as the news spread that a man might just survive in a shack on the shore in the rain, while his buddy froze to death in a similar shelter on the bleak, bald plains.

Already the coast was crowded with its own quota of unemployed. Already mills stood idle and quiet without the whine of the gang saws. Already the canneries lay rotting in the rain while worms worked on their underpinnings. Already the mines loomed like stark, empty tombs of rock where no powder blasted the ore with a blinding flash and angry roar.

Still the men poured westwards. They came down the angry rushing Fraser Canyon on the top of flat cars; in open rattling box cars; wrapped in rags; chilled to their marrow, hoping to find a hovel that would somehow keep off the eternal rain.

The plight of these drifters weighed heavily on the heart of the Missionary who felt something must be done and done soon.

In Port Alberni the men were sleeping under bleachers—they shacked up in tumbled down shelters built of driftwood, tar paper, and scrap metal. Some just covered themselves with cardboard and resigned themselves to fate.

But even this did not deter others from coming. They were crowded on the highways, some on foot, others driving old rattletrap jalopies held together with binder twine, haywire and black tape.

To make their plight more pitiful the local police chivied and chased these broken men from town to town—but still their numbers rose to dangerous proportions and this caused civic problems. No one would shoulder responsibility for the drifters. From town—to province—to federal government—the buck was passed with no one really to blame.

This was the depression—the bitter fruit of the destitute which every community tasted to greater or less degree.

Finally the Missionary could endure the atrocious state of affairs no longer. He approached the town fathers and asked, "Why don't you do something for these men?"

This question was sidestepped neatly, by passing the responsibility to the Province.

Then one of their leaders countered with the remark: "Well, if you're so concerned—why don't you do something?"

"Give me a plot of ground—and I will," the Missionary shot back.

So he was given a lot, well-littered with the usual accumulation of logs, stumps, rusty cans and old junked cars that are so often a heritage of western frontier towns.

The next morning in the grey drizzle the Missionary went and stood upon this plot of ground. He saw beyond the stumps, the tin cans, the skeletons of rusting cars. He saw here a buiding that would shelter, feed and comfort men in distress. He dreamed of building, not just to build, but to bring honour to God. He claimed by faith the hearts and lives of men who would come here broken in spirit, but who would leave, born again from above—regenerated in body and mind by the touch of the Master's Hand.

And so with this vision in mind, he lifted his heart to God as he stood there alone that morning. This is what he prayed: "Oh God—because this work is to bring glory to Yourself, confirm it this morning by sending someone here with money so we can start to build." Scarcely had the words been breathed, when he heard a car grating along the gravel road behind him. It pulled to a stop and the driver called out to him, "Is that you, my friend?"

"Yes it's me!" the Missionary replied, recognizing the man's voice at once.

"Why didn't you come to see me?" the driver called, beckoning him to the car.

"I just got in yesterday," the Missionary replied, going over and getting in the front seat. "And anyway I've been busy."

"I've got a cheque waiting for you in my office; come on down and I'll give it to you!"

The two men drove to the office, and there sure enough was a cheque already made out to him for fifty dollars—which in those days was a fine chunk of money.

God had confirmed the work. He had shown Himself faithful to His servant.

The men conversed for a short time, then the missionary made bold to enquire of his friend, who was the manager of the local mill: "How does my rating stand with you people? I want to start building up on that lot!"

"Go down to the lumber piles," the manager waved in their direction. "My foreman will fix you up."

The foreman led him through the piles, selecting load upon load of what in those days was considered cull lumber, but which today would grade number two or three.

"If you can get a truck down here in a hurry—you can take all you want at five dollars a thousand before the boss changes his mind!"

A truck was soon rounded up and load upon load of lumber for the building went to the lot.

So "The Stranger's Rest" was born. In its first eighteen months of operation, over 11,000 men went through its doors.

When he would drop into the "Rest" from time to time on his travels the Missionary would find as many as 36 men at a time sleeping in a room. Some under the tables, some on the tables, others on the floor, on chairs—anywhere at all to be out of the rain and cold.

Yet no man passed through that place without being presented boldly with the claim of Christ upon his life. So it became widely known as a Gospel center as well as welfare post.

As pointed out earlier, in connection with the early establishment of the hospital, the Shantymen do not operate or financially support permanent endeavors of this sort. A Shanty boy is essentially a roving missionary, bearing to wayside individuals the Gospel message.

However, in both of these instances, when a need became apparent, the Missionary would not hesitate to do all in his power, under the direction of God's Spirit, to meet the emergency. Once the enterprise was launched and under way, then of course its operation and support would be turned over to other hands. Meanwhile he would lend his utmost encouragement to the cause both spiritually, morally, and in any other way God directed him.

In essence, then, each of these endeavors became an entirely separate and independent entity. They were entrusted to the care of others and to the tender mercy of Almighty God. In His abundant goodness, God has richly blessed not only the medical work and this welfare work over the years, but also the little churches, the servicemen's work, the children's work and the boats, all of which had their original concept in the mind of this Missionary.

It is a measure of this man that he lays no initial claim to being responsible for the success of these endeavours. Yet to those closely acquainted with each, it is common knowledge that without his vision, without his enormous will and enthusiasm, without his unflinching faith in the unfaltering faithfulness of Almighty God, many of the West Coast people would have missed much. His shining spirit, his unbounded generosity, set this man apart from the general run of men in Christian work, and God has rewarded his devotion a hundred times over.

It would be quite beyond the scope of this book to attempt a resumé of all that has transpired across the years at "The Stranger's Rest." Sufficient to say that here uncounted numbers of men have found a new will to live; have been fed, clothed, housed and above all brought into a practical, living relationship with the Master.

One account of the manner in which this outpost has been used by God will bear witness to its worth, and help to convince some sceptics of the invincible power of prayer.

In later years, a Union Hall was built adjacent to "The Stranger's Rest." Anyone familiar with the life of loggers, miners and fishermen knows that such men are not dainty daisies. They are rowdy, hurly-burly fellows who, when they get a drink under their belt, or a peeve in their pocket, take a perverted delight in throwing their weight around to the discomfort of everyone else.

During the strikes, sit-downs, or shutdowns which are the warp and woof of a logger's life in the west, this Union Hall became a gathering point for all the malcontents and die-hards of the district.

Night after night the place would rock under the pounding feet of dancing crowds. Its walls would shake with the shouts of garrulous gangs. Hard liquor would be firing up spirits and shortening tempers until bedlam reigned into the late hours of the night.

In this crowd there stood out one tough, rough character who assumed leadership of his gang. Night after night his boys would come outside the hall, hurl their beer bottles against "The Stranger's Rest," and curse the place from the heights of Heaven to the deepest Hell.

It was a nerve-shattering business for the folks who manned the "Rest."

Sleep was impossible. A terrible din, with its continuous stream of profanity and obscenity that engulfed them, began to fray nerves and bring on drab despair.

About this time the Missionary appeared on the scene. He was told about the state of affairs. It lay upon his heart as a great burden. Especially did he feel constrained to pray that this gang leader should be won for God.

The rows continued. The dancing never abated. The beer bottles continued to shatter against the walls. Those in the "Rest" became more perturbed.

Amongst the roughnecks there was also a flaming-eyed woman zealot who left no stone unturned in her tirades and attacks on the Gospel witness. As is commonly known there is no one tougher than a tough woman—and this "gal" was no exception.

The Missionary gathered a select group of Christians in the village and most earnest prayer was offered that God Himself would intervene in a situation utterly beyond human means.

Suddenly the tide of affairs turned. God's Spirit began to move in the leader's heart. He became disturbed in mind. A great conviction came upon him. To use his own words he was enduring a veritable Hell of his own manufacture.

After two days he could stand it no longer. A broken, penitent man, he stumbled into the "Rest" asking that they should pray for him. He longed for deliverance and relief from his torment of soul. God in His unfailing mercy, came and met him with pardon. His conversion was a glorious rebirth—a total surrender of life and will to Christ.

Marvel of marvels—a few days later, who should follow him but the wild woman who had been such a terror. She too met the Saviour in absolute contrition and repentance.

Between these two young Christians a friendship quickly sprang up. The friendship blossomed, then ripened into the full fruit of rich, deep Christian love.

Not long after "The Stranger's Rest" was brightly festooned with streamers and ornaments. There the Missionary was invited to join this couple as man and wife in a colourful marriage ceremony.

To this day theirs is a godly home. Into it later came a child who was held in the strong arms of the Missionary as with joyous heart he dedicated him to God.

The vision God had given him that morning as he stood looking over an empty lot cluttered with stumps, cans, and broken cars had come to vibrant life.

God is good! He will not mock those who trust Him!

The Doctor's Call to the Coast

D URING THOSE PIONEER YEARS that the Missionary was working, both in the backwoods of Northern Alberta, and on
the West Coast of the Island, God had been carefully grooming
another man for medical work on "The Graveyard of the Pacific."

This young man, who had been reared in a godly farm home
in Manitoba, returned from the first world war—intent on training to become a civil engineer. Through the influence of friends
at the University, and no doubt too because God already had
a special work planned for him, he changed his mind and went
into medicine. This at the time seemed a most unlikely career
for one who, to quote his own words "fainted at the very sight
of blood, while to be a surgeon was unthinkable!"

Nonetheless by sheer dint of perseverance and practice his
medical course was completed after ten long years of struggling
to pay his way through college. No small part of the credit
for this achievement goes to the Doctor's young wife who by

her thrift, self-effacing life and hard work during these difficult
years enabled him to obtain his degree. During his studies he
had felt a compelling desire to engage in mission work of some
sort. Through the Student Volunteer Missionary Movement on
the campus he offered himself for service to the church. Because of his age—he was now over 30 and married—his application was rejected.

The life of David Livingstone in Africa had made an immense
impression on his heart. Especially did he feel that any man
who died praying on his knees as Livingstone had, on behalf
of the "dark continent," was worthy to be followed. It is not
surprising that during the ensuing years there persisted within
him an eager desire to go to Africa.

Upon graduation an opportunity suddenly presented itself
for him to take over the lucrative practice of an elderly doctor
who was retiring from the small town of Togo in Northern Saskatchewan. In spite of the attractive income, he was loath to
go there unless he could also find missionary activity to occupy
him in the community. In this he was most fortunate to meet
the local minister, Rev. Herman McConnel, from the same
town, who assured him that he himself would be glad to give
him all he could do in his spare time what with speaking appointments, choir work, and a host of other church functions.

In this manner the first year passed very rapidly for he was
busy healing bodies and doing his first mission work. Business
was brisk and he and his wife enjoyed living in their fine home
on a then splendid income of over four hundred dollars a
month.

Suddenly on the very morning that their eldest daughter was
born the whole picture altered in a matter of hours. A wire
came from the headquarters of the church to which he had
originally applied for mission service as a student, offering him
a post at Bella Coola amongst the Indians on the Pacific Coast—
but at less than half the salary he was now getting.

This was an exciting moment for the Doctor. So exciting that
he could not withhold the news from his wife who felt groggy
just after the delivery of her child. Prospects of such a shift in

their life pattern was hardly the sort of thing to lift a woman's spirits at such a critical moment.

Within six weeks of receiving the wire, the Doctor had disposed of his practice and moved his family out to the coast. Exactly one year from the day he started his practice in Northern Saskatchewan, he set up his office at Bella Coola—which it should be remembered is on the West Coast of the mainland of British Columbia and has no connection with Vancouver Island or the work of the Shantymen on the West Coast of Vancouver Island.

On his arrival at Bella Coola, one of the local residents asked him outright if he thought he could stick it out any longer than his predecessors—of whom there had been eight doctors in seven years. This did nothing to cheer his wife who visualized herself shifting from this home again in a few months.

But the Doctor was made of stern stuff and for seven years he worked diligently both in his hospital and in any missionary endeavour that presented itself. This latter exercise appeared to irk the church, more especially since it was not considered part of his duty. His continual insistence, too, that some day he wished to go to Africa, made his position more and more difficult, even though he had learned to love the Indians and enjoyed the respect of the entire community.

Eventually a parting of the ways came. Feeling that he was not yet fully fitted for the mission service which was so dear to his heart, he decided to take a year of Bible study at the Prairie Bible Institute in Three Hills, Alberta.

At Bella Coola he had learned the secret of praying with patience on behalf of his patients. At the institute his spiritual experience was a deepening growth in the knowledge and understanding of God's Word. For him this was a winter of joyous refreshment in spirit and soul—a time of seeking diligently for God's guidance in his career.

He would pray earnestly, "Oh, God, if you can't send me to Africa—then let me go to the toughest place on the West Coast!"

God was to take him up on his request. For it was the next spring, while doing postgraduate work at the General Hospital

Dept. of Recreation and Conservation, Victoria, B.C., Canada
Fishboats

A Contented Fisherman with Spring Salmon

Dept. of Recreation and Conservation, Victoria, B.C., Canada

Setting Out to Sea *Government of B.C., Canada*

Fishermen Mending Nets

Government of B.C., Canada

in Vancouver, that a wire came for him one Friday from the Shantyman Missionary in Victoria. It was an invitation for him to come over on Sunday for the annual Shantymen's day of prayer.

Now neither man knew the other up to this time, but the Missionary, having heard of the Doctor who prayed for God to send him to the toughest spot on the West Coast, felt convinced that he knew where it was—and would gladly show it to him— plumb in the centre of "The Graveyard of the Pacific."

The Doctor, who up to this point had never experienced the walk of simple faith in God's provision for his daily needs, suddenly took the first step by stating that he would not go to Victoria unless God somehow supplied his boat fare and thus made clear that this was the thing for him to do.

On Saturday, coming out of the hospital, three Hindus stopped him on the steps. They saw his white coat, asked him if he would come into the room where an aged relative was dying, and help them write out a will in English.

This he did gladly, for he was fond of all dark-skinned people.

When they were through the men turned and asked, "Do you smoke?"

"No," was the answer with a grin.

"Well, then, you can use the money for anything you like!"

"What money?" he thought to himself—not knowing exactly what they meant. Just then he glanced down and saw that in typical oriental style, they had stuffed his big coat pocket with paper money. Here there was more than to spare for his voyage to Victoria.

The next day he sailed on the crowded Canadian Pacific Railway boat not knowing quite how he could identify the Missionary who would be waiting for him at the dock. Yet without a moment's hesitation the two men were instantly attracted to each other and thus met to commence an intimate comradeship that has never flagged over twenty-five years.

The Doctor was deeply impressed by the meeting of the Shantymen. Surely God was there in great power. Afterwards the Missionary turned to him. "How about going up the West

Coast of the Island with me? I have made plans to leave in 'Messenger II' at 1:00 P.M. on Monday—one week from to-morrow!"

The Doctor said he would have to check on getting leave from the hospital. The Missionary assured him God could easily care for such trifles. Sure enough the hospital superintendent assured him the following week would be ideal for him to go. So a week later he was back in Victoria with the Missionary.

By this time there was a tremendous turmoil in the Doctor's mind over whether or not he should go to Africa or become deeply interested in the West Coast again. That morning as he and the Missionary drove out to Sidney to call on friends, he pleaded with God to reveal His will for his lifework.

"If you want me on the West Coast, Lord," he cried, "confirm it by providing a place for my family to live this summer."

In the three and a half hours at their disposal the men visited seven families that afternoon. Before returning home they dropped in at the first house they had visited for a final fare-well.

"By the way," the lady of the house remarked quite casually, "since you were here a few hours ago, God has told me to offer you and your family the use of our furnished home for the summer. You can have the garden, too; it is all planted."

There was the answer he wanted! Without any delay he wired his wife to come from Alberta as soon as it could be arranged.

But if God had thus intimated the field to which his attention was to be drawn for the summer, He was yet to put an absolute seal upon His explicit instructions to go to the Coast. For up till now the Doctor felt he was merely exploring the ground.

When the two men rose early the next morning the Missionary turned to the Doctor and asked if he could borrow five cents to buy a bottle of milk for breakfast. This small act was almost the Doctor's utter undoing. "After all," he thought to himself, "what kind of an outfit is this I'm getting in with? Here we are due to sail at one o'clock. The cupboards are bare; not even enough money to buy a quart of milk; then this missionary tells me to look to God for my daily provision. Why can't he do it himself?"

These were the normal, usual, human impulses that would come to anyone in similar circumstances—especially one who had not yet proved the great, unchanging faithfulness of God in every area of life.

After a meagre breakfast the Missionary asked him if he had brought along his instruments and medical supplies for the journey.

"Me!" he ejaculated. "Why of course not—all my things are still stored back at the Institute in Alberta!"

"Well, then let's pray about it," the Missionary replied, and the two men kneeled in the cabin of "Messenger II."

After prayer the Doctor was asked if he had any leading from God as to what he should do. He only shook his head in reply.

Just then the Missionary looked out the porthole and saw a Red Cross sign painted on a building in the town.

"Go up there," he remarked pointing out the place. "Maybe they'll give you some bandages and dressings to take along."

The Doctor went up and made enquiry of the ladies at the depot. He got only a sad shake of the head: "If you wanted us to dress a cut or bind some small wound that would be different! But bandages!"

They must have detected his downcast countenance for one asked if he would care to call the Red Cross superintendent on the telephone to see what he would say. This he did, and the man on the line very nearly bit his head off for daring to be so bold. He was on the point of hanging up the phone when the superintendent suddenly asked, "Could you see me now?"

He said he could, and the two men arranged to meet at one of the leading druggists in town.

The superintendent asked him to select the supplies he thought he could use from the assorted display hanging on the walls of the store. This he did with gusto, including such expensive items as a blood pressure machine, oralscope and other instruments.

Finally there were boxes and boxes of medicines, drugs, bandages, and dressings. All were added to a list which by now was worth well over $150.00. In the Doctor's mind a touch of consternation was coming to the surface: "But who will pay for all this?"

He turned and put the question to the superintendent.

"Charge it to the Red Cross," he replied.

The Red Cross account—"Charge it to the Red Cross!" The words were doubly significant to the Doctor. More than just these supplies had been charged to that account—the whole of man's iniquity could be charged to the account of the Cross— and that would be the message of his life on the coast. This was God's Word to him. Now there could be no further doubt!

Elated over this remarkable demonstration of God's provision, the Doctor went back and jumped on the boat, bubbling over with excitement.

When he had finished recounting what had taken place the Missionary turned to him and said, "Just look around this boat and see what else God has done while you were gone."

The food lockers were full; parcels and packages were stored under the bunks; the gas tanks had been filled and the Missionary had money on hand to purchase further supplies up the coast.

At one o'clock as had been scheduled more than a month before, the little "Messenger II" put out to sea. God had prepared a timetable and they were right on schedule. On board was the Doctor who had embarked on much more than just a sea voyage—but also a life of utter faith in God for every emergency.

The first few days were ghastly for the Doctor. The rocking, rolling, pitching boat made him violently ill. The Missionary, a man of many parts, prepared what, for himself, were delightful dishes of oatmeal, figs, nuts, and raisins, but which to the good Doctor were abominable concoctions of monstrous proportions.

Finally in utter desperation one day, he shouted out, "If I

want porridge I want porridge—if I want pudding I want pudding! But not the two mixed!"

Everywhere the two men went, the need for medical aid was overwhelming. Port Renfrew, Bamfield, Hecate—almost every stop they made, the local people begged the Doctor to stay and be their resident physician. The farther north they went the more obvious became the appalling condition of the West Coast. No doctor, no nurses, no hospital, no telephone, only suffering men and women.

"This is the place God wants me!" the Doctor finally declared one night when they moored near Hecate. In the little cabin of the boat the Missionary assured him that he would give him every kind of moral and spiritual support that was possible. His financial backing, however, was a matter between himself and God. So there were brought into being the first stages of a mission hospital and a medical marine work to serve "The Graveyard of the Pacific."

The Doctor had come—TO STAY.

Launching a Hospital

CONVINCED NOW, beyond any thought of doubting, that the time had arrived to establish a permanent medical work on the coast, the Missionary set out in a small rowboat to explore the shore line in this immediate vicinity for a suitable building site.

It was not long before he found what he was looking for. Just to the west of Ceepeecee in Hecate Channel there was a fairly level bench of land that jutted from the mountainside out into the sea. A fine stream of pure mountain water tumbled down across this spot. Best of all it stood on a southern exposure where every particle of sunshine—and goodness knows there is precious little of it on the West Coast—could warm and cheer the place.

In spite of the fact that they did not yet have legal possession of the land on which they were planning to build—it was decided that time was too precious to waste that first summer and they would start anyway and run the risk of being turned down in their application for the site. Meanwhile they would put the first building on skids, so that it could be dragged off if worse came to worst.

The arrival of these men in the area did not meet altogether with the openhearted reception that had been shown them by isolated individuals here and there. The liquor interests, mill bosses and mine operators who capitalized on the appetite of their men for alcohol, and the relative isolation of their western domain, took a dim view of these determined newcomers. In fact some of them made so bold as to declare they would "drive the Gospel off the Coast."

One night while exploring the area, they had lying in one of their bunks on the boat an old prospector who had injured his knee and had come to them for relief. Another young logger came in with an infected hand that night, asking for treatment. The poison had already run up his arm and was in its last critical stages. The Doctor realized at once that with his limited facilities on board suitable treatment was impossible and so ordered him to take the mail boat down to Alberni and the hospital there next morning.

The logger was penniless, except for a worthless cheque from his logging outfit which had gone broke, because its boss drank himself into bankruptcy. Seeing the logger's plight the Doctor went over to the little Oxo box in which all their missionary funds were kept and finding only nine dollars left there, dumped the entire contents into the man's hand and told him to jump on the mail boat and get going.

So when the two men knelt in prayer that morning to seek God's guidance for the next step in their work—and remember, here they were planning a hospital—it was with an empty kitty. Not one cent did they have. They felt led to cross the channel to a little mill at McBride Bay to see what it would cost to put up a building the size of a normal bunkhouse, about 14' × 32'. As they walked down through the lumber piles they bumped into the foreman. He had a terrific hangover from carousing the night before. When told what they wanted the lumber for, he exploded into a tirade of profanity, stating that he would have nothing to do with any mission building.

The men were not to be frightened or put off. Finally he told them to come back in half an hour. When they did the foreman himself was not there but they met the manager instead.

"How soon do you want to start?" he asked.

"This morning," they replied.

"Alright," he answered, anxious to get rid of them, "I'll give you the stuff if you'll get it out of here this morning."

With a strength born in the heat of victory, the men simply dumped the lumber in the bay, lashed it into bundles, and towed it across the water to their site with "Messenger II." The hospital was under way!

It so happened that there was a fish camp close by at Hecate just then, and the men who were out of work gladly came down and helped with the building. To compensate them the Doctor agreed to pay for their meals at the bunkhouse at summer's end.

By August the building was pretty well completed and little by little the Doctor began to equip and furnish it as best he could. Most of this time now he was working alone, for the Missionary had gone on with "Messenger II' calling on the isolated folk.

Before the Missionary left, the Doctor suggested that they should sit down and write to a number of nurses who might be interested in coming to help in the new work. To this the Missionary replied, "No, Doc. God already knows the nurses He wants up here—He'll send them."

Finally one late, dark evening as summer moved into fall, the Doctor decided to cross the channel from Hecate in his own boat to take over the last load of his belongings to the hospital.

He had not yet had any patients there while he was working on the building. But on this night in the darkness a sudden autumn squall of wind and rain came up from the southeast. It blew him northwards up the channel towards Zeballos, in the dark. He was hugging the mountainside rowing like mad until he noticed a large black rock emerge from the night. He was driven onto this and had a grim struggle to free himself, out-fitted as he was in heavy gum boots and oilskins.

At last he broke the boat loose, leaped into it and rowed hard down the shore back towards the hospital. Finally he found it at the base of its towering mountain which could just barely be seen outlined against the night sky.

As he was wading ashore, dragging the boat up the beach, a blinding beam reached out to him from a powerful spotlight across the channel. The light was aimed at the hospital build-ing and through the surge of the sea and the whine of wind in the trees overhead he heard a boat approaching. It was a wicked night for anyone to be out and why was anyone coming to his hospital at that hour?

When the boat neared shore, its searchlight picked up the doctor draped in his rain clothes and boots, standing in the pouring rain.

"Is the Doctor there?" a voice shouted.

"Yes," came the reply, "what do you want?"

"We've got a man on board, nearly dead!"

"Bring him in!" the Doctor shouted above the storm. This was to be his first patient. Again God's timetable was precisely on time for the Doctor had been assured that the hospital would open November 1, 1937, and this was the very night.

The logger had an immense swollen gland under his arm, which in a few hours would have taken his life when its dis-charge of poison reached the heart. An immediate operation was inevitable.

"One of you fellows will have to administer the anaesthetic for me," the Doctor remarked, as he started to fashion a home-made mask from wire with a pair of pliers.

All but one of the burly loggers headed for the door when

he said this. ' Under compulsion one, younger and more daring than the others, stayed behind and agreed to help in the operation.

In the light of the Doctor's small head lamp, the gland was lanced and an ugly dark mass of pus, flowed out and over the floor. By the time the wound was all cleaned up, midnight had nearly struck. But the man was resting in ease and quietness.

From that epic night, the icy coldness of the local people towards the Doctor thawed. Men came to him from far and near. His reputation spread up and down the coast as only it can in such out-of-the-way places, and to this day a steady flow of patients has come to his doors.

Nor had God forgotten about nurses. That fall a fully trained nurse felt urged to offer her services to the work. At the same time another friend of hers felt a call to the coast, so the two decided to come together.

A young man, too, who had heard of the pioneer effort felt he wanted to share in it. Unbeknown to any of the others he too came along at the very same hour and boarded the identical boat on which not only were the two nurses travelling, but also the Doctor's wife and family who had been separated from him all this time.

Imagine the utter elation and overflowing joy with which he met the old Canadian Pacific Railway's "Maquinna" that November day, when it arrived with all these reinforcements for the work.

The hospital was launched—and under way!

Sailing in Troubled Waters

ANY MAN AND WORK established under the Hand of Almighty God must, if they are to endure, be put to severe test. Not only does this hardening process fit the man and work for future hardships, but most important of all it enables God Himself to demonstrate His own unwavering trustworthiness under every adversity.

The little Esperanza hospital—for it was named "Esperanza" meaning "the place of hope"—though away to a flying start that first year of its history, was soon to encounter troubled waters—both literal and figurative.

On Thursday, December 2, 1937, the faithful old C.P.R. "Maquinna" came steaming into Port Alberni with the provincial land inspector on board. The Missionary happened to be in Port Alberni at the time, and that evening decided to go down and visit the ship. There he met an old friend called Shorty who tipped him off that the land inspector was on board with instructions to sell the government lands surveyed at Zeballos and Esperanza. It was on Lot 2 of the latter that the little hospital stood.

It will be remembered that the hospital had been erected without owning the land. Subsequently, however, the government had shown sufficient interest in the project to assure the men that their application for the site would be granted. Now suddenly out of a blue sky, without any prior notice the land was being put on the auction block. Not having any funds in hand for such a purchase it looked as though the hospital had reached a sudden end.

In great haste the Missionary dashed off a note that would be carried on board the "Maquinna," advising the Doctor to get up to Zeballos on Monday, December 6, to bid on Lot 2 anyway, which was to go at $200.00 to the first bidder. God would supply money somehow! Then that night he got down upon his knees seeking guidance for what next step should be taken. The following morning he called on an old friend in the town who had been a surveyor on the coast. He offered to loan the Missionary money for the purchase price. To this the Missionary demurred.

"No—this is to be a time when God Himself will deliver us from this extremity."

The surveyor suggested that they meet a local lawyer the next morning, Saturday. This they did, relating to him the entire history of the hospital.

He was a quiet, soft-spoken man, and after listening to the case, turned to the Missionary and said, "What were you doing before you came up here this morning?"

"I was chopping wood down at the 'Stranger's Rest.'"

"Well," he drawled with a twinkle in his eye, "you go back to chopping wood—and don't worry."

The Missionary went back to his woodpile, wondering what would happen now. Just before noon a wire was delivered to him from the Minister of Lands in Victoria. It read simply: "I have instructed our inspector to withdraw Lot 2 from the land sale."

Of course his delight was unbounded as he saw the words on the yellow slip of paper.

On board "Maquinna," however, an altogether different mood prevailed in the inspector's stateroom. When the Missionary had come in to see him about the sale while the ship was docked in Alberni, he had been most officious and dictatorial in his attitude—remarking in an offhand manner that if they wanted the land they would have to get up to Zeballos and buy it—that was all.

Suddenly on the weekend in Ceepeecee he had received instructions to withdraw this lot from the sale. This was the first time there had been any such reversal of policy in his thirty-five years of service, and he was furious.

To add insult to injury the Doctor, at this crucial juncture, burst in upon him, waving a sheaf of cheques, insisting that he would gladly buy the land before anyone else could bid on it.

To understand this we must go back a little to where the Doctor met the "Maquinna" at Ceepeecee on Saturday to get his mail. The first letter he opened was from the Missionary, and naturally he was dumbfounded, for he hadn't a cent with which to buy the property, so how could he bid on it?

Yet wonder of wonders, for the first time since he had been up on the coast, letter after letter in that same mail, on the very same boat that carried the inspector, bore cheques for him, with more than ample to buy the land . . . to be exact $310.00 came in that very day.

Little wonder he rushed in to see the inspector with such enthusiasm! The inspector, for his part, realizing by this time that the game was up no matter what he did—for either way the hospital was saved under the provision of God's Hand—changed his entire attitude and befriended the Doctor.

He even went on to assist him in securing a choice building site in Zeballos for an outpost—besides arranging that the land at Esperanza be leased for a twenty-one-year period at the nominal sum of one dollar a year! How good is God!

It was some considerable time after this that the inspector ran into the Missionary one day in the Provincial buildings at Victoria.

He seized him by the shoulder and in a stern voice demanded:

"Who have you got in Victoria pulling strings for you in the Government?"

To this the Missionary replied: "No one but God, who answers prayer."

It was shortly after this exciting episode that the same Shorty who had tipped off the missionary about the land sale, was making a trip to Victoria, and invited the Doctor to go along for a free ride.

The night before they set out, the Doctor had a most vivid dream that he was outside his little shack at the hospital, when he saw money scattered about on the ground. He started to gather it up, counting the bills as he did so. The sum ran up to $1,036.00 . . . $1,037.00 . . . then suddenly ended as he woke.

Together with Shorty he went to Victoria, met the Missionary, and attended a small gathering of Shantymen who had assembled to try and raise a little love offering for his hospital.

The sum they gathered was very modest, about $50.00. Nonetheless for depression days a very acceptable gift. Just as he was going out the door a little lady came up to him and pressed $20.00 into his hands.

"Wow," he thought to himself, "that's a lot for one lady!" and thanked her profusely.

The next morning the phone rang where he was staying and the same little lady was on the phone again. "Do you remember me giving you $20.00 at the door last night?" she queried in a tremulous voice.

Indeed he did—how could he forget!

"Well," she went on hesitantly, "last night God spoke to me in the meeting, telling me to give you the entire $900.00 I had in the bank. But I thought I could just get by with giving you $20.00. I can't. Please accept the balance of $880.00 this morning."

This was almost beyond belief. Here he had scarcely been in the city twenty-four hours, and already he had received nearly $1000.00 in gifts.

A little later he called on his old friends at Sidney, and they too showered kindness on him.

Then he counted up what had come in. It was precisely the amount of $1,037.00 that he had dreamed about.

With this he purchased a small boat for work out of the hospital to be called the "Dieu Donné"—"The Gift of God"—for so it was in very truth. He was also able to procure an X ray machine, and other essential equipment for his infant work.

It was a gay and lighthearted Doctor that returned to the little hospital perched at the foot of its rugged mountain after that trip.

But the "Dieu Donné" was destined to have a short though colourful career on the coast. It was in her that the bighearted, indefatigable Doctor who drove himself night and day for his people, came to be well known up and down the coast.

About nine months later, he was away from the hospital, when a group of his small staff took the boat to Zeballos. On board were the head nurse—a great woman of prayer—her two assistants, and an engineer. At Zeballos a stranger—a logger—asked to join them on the return trip. To this they consented, so that there were two men and three ladies on board.

They left Zeballos about 4:30 P.M. in November with dark clouds, threatening skies, and a wind from the west starting to blow.

Conditions got steadily worse as they sailed down the channel, with mean squalls gusting from off the Pacific. About one third of the way home the manifold on the motor blew up, threatening to set the boat on fire and engulf them in flames.

In desperation the engineer shut off the engine, in order to save the craft from burning. Now lying helpless in the rising seas, the waves started to drive them towards the rocks on shore. It would only be a matter of moments until the boat would be battered on the boulders and founder.

The nurse cried to God for deliverance out of danger. She prayed that the wind would change. And it did.

To their utter amazement the seas changed direction and drove the boat back up against the main current into the mouth of the Little Zeballos River, where she ran aground on a bar in midstream.

Perhaps in sheer desperation, or maybe with less wisdom than calm consideration, in order to try and free the boat, the engi-

neer attempted to start the motor again in spite of the fire
hazard. The old engine backfired so violently it knocked him
over and laid him out.

By this hour there was almost total darkness. The stranger
who was with them, thought he could now make out the
shore near at hand. Bravely he plunged overboard and discovered that he could touch the bottom and wade through the
water that reached to his armpits.

To his astonishment he found that they had grounded close
to the only beach he knew of in that entire area. Going ashore
he discovered an old prospector's log cabin on the shore. Quickly he smashed off the lock with a rock, groped in the darkness
for matches, dry kindling, and wood. Soon he had a fire going.

In the pitch blackness of night he waded back out to the
stranded boat, and one at a time carried the three women (two
of whom each weighed 200 pounds) and the injured man
through the waves and up to the cabin. All of them were soaked
through, and chilled to the marrow, for rain and sloshing seas
had washed into the boat until it lay low in the water and the
occupants could find no refuge from the chill water.

In the log cabin there was food, a little dry clothing and some
old blankets. With these meagre comforts the little band
cheered themselves and waited out the night.

The next morning the sturdy logger set out on foot for Zeballos to find help. He plunged into the dripping salal and soaked
ferns of the rain-sodden forest and climbed over the high mountains that separated the little beach from the nearest human
beings. For four hours he fought his way through the track-
less tangle of that wicked west coast timber, until he found
help.

Two men volunteered to bring their boats along in an attempt
to refloat the "Dieu Donné." The sea was still wild and before
ever they reached her one of their craft foundered and sank
in the storm.

The remaining boat managed to get a line aboard the "Dieu
Donné" and towed her clear. However, she was so badly beaten
by the pounding seas, that though she returned to the hospital

Dept. of Recreation and Conservation, Victoria, B.C., Canada
Indian Carver

THE STALWARTS
"The Doctor"—"The Missionary"—"The Skipper"

"The Skipper" Samples a Morsel of his Smoked Salmon

never again was she put into service. So it was that in His great providence, God saw fit to have that strong logger, an utter stranger, accompany the hospital folk on this particular mission.

In His great mercy too, the elements were made to alter the direction of their fury and so drive the craft close to the only beach with the only cabin along that entire bit of bleak and hostile coastline.

Anywhere else, the boat would have been shattered on the rocks, probably with the loss of all lives on board.

After this the next little boat to enter the hospital service was named "Elizabeth." She served faithfully and sturdily for almost nine years.

Then when her usefulness was past, there was donated to the hospital that grand old girl "Messenger II."

In the intervening years, "Messenger II" had sailed many thousands of miles under another master, the Skipper—who now enters our story for the first time.

The Skipper

THERE ARE, quite obviously, scores and scores of skippers on the Pacific Coast—but to anyone who knows anything at all about the Shantymen or their marine activities—there is only one man by the name of the "Skipper." More often than not, too, he is known as "Our beloved Skipper." Nor is this title lightly won—for during the twenty-odd years that he has skippered the Shantymen's boats over the "Graveyard of the Pacific" he has won the love and devotion of almost everyone whose path he has crossed.

Like the Missionary and the Doctor who preceded him in this work, there had been a long period of preparation for the precise niche he was to fill in the Shantymen endeavour. This is always God's method of equipping the men he intends to use in accomplishing His purposes.

Nothing happens by chance or caprice. Rather, each experience is intended to serve as the sculptor's chisel shaping men to the precise pattern God has in mind.

The Skipper's birthplace and boyhood home were on Vancouver Island—nor across the years has he ever moved far from these Pacific shores. In fact he is one of those men with a share of salt water in his veins and the West's blue skies in his eyes.

Though he grew up in a God-fearing home, his life was not

entirely entrusted to the Master, until later years. From that time on he held a deep interest in children and especially in attempting to win young folk for God, before age and the adversities of life turned their hearts hard in the struggle to earn a living.

It was between the two world wars, that much of the Skipper's time was to be spent on the Union boats that made their way up and down the West Coast, from Vancouver to Alaska and around the Queen Charlotte Islands. He had signed on with the Union Steamship Company as a waiter during the first war, and this later was switched for a steward's job.

About this time the dreadful flu epidemic of the first great war was sweeping through the ships, and on his particular boat two quartermasters went down with it. Both these men were packed ashore—never to return—for they died of the disease.

In desperation, one night, the master of the ship came down and grabbed this lad as a substitute. He showed him into the wheelhouse, and set to work teaching him to steer by compass in the inky blackness of night. It was somewhat of a terrifying ordeal for a boy not twenty, to try and hold a ship on course down such a treacherous stretch of water as Johnston Narrows. Here the ebb and flow of the swirling tides made the ship swing and sway in the current, so that to keep on compass was a most tantalizing and tricky business.

The sturdy fellow weathered this ordeal and rapidly won the confidence of his superiors who were quick to note his cool bearing and self-control under the pressure of danger.

For many years he delighted in his career, and felt very much at home in boats and on the sea. When recounting some of those times he makes the remark that the usual custom then was to stand six hours on watch, then six off, followed by six more on. But on "Messenger III"—working for God—it is not too unusual to be on duty sixteen hours steady. Such is the dedication of those who go down to the sea in ships for their lost fellowmen.

This, he is quick to point out, is not because of any natural human inclination—but rather because the desire and interest to reach isolated men and women is a God-implanted interest in the heart.

Again and again he has been heard to remark, while sailing past an isolated logging camp or fishing village—which time would not permit him to visit on that particular trip, "My, if only a man had several lives to live, that he could spend calling in at every one of these homes and cabins. There is hardly one that does not have a burden or tangled problem that God could help—If only we could get in there with His Word!"

This deep, honest, sincere concern for the people of the coast is one of his shining attributes, that can never be hidden behind his humble, shy and retiring character.

Perhaps because this man has lived for so long in company with danger as his bedfellow, there has grown upon him a profound sense of dependence upon God's guidance in every emergency. To those who have sailed and worked with him it is patent that the skipper is continually led by God's Spirit in even the smallest decisions which are made from one moment to the next in his dangerous mission.

The need for such a simple trust in God for guidance, may well have been instilled deep in his mind by several harrowing experiences he had before joining the Shantymen. One night, coming out of Vancouver harbour in a heavy fog, the ship on which he was then first mate, suddenly collided with a large steamer. For some reason, the ship's captain had ordered full speed ahead a few minutes before, so that they were now travelling at maximum velocity when the impact occurred.

Their ship struck the other steamer with such a tremendous impact, about thirty feet back from the bow, that the smaller boat was literally thrown sideways by her own momentum, crashing again full length alongside the larger vessel. The two successive blows threw men off their feet; hurled some of the engine-room crew to the floor where they were seriously injured, and left the ship heavily disabled.

In such moments a man needs a cool head, to ascertain whether one is taking water and going down—whether injured men require first aid—and what immediate steps should be taken to save the ship.

In this case the vessel was saved, but the extent of damages ran to $70,000.00, which in the depression days was a formidable figure indeed.

Subsequent to this he tells of another occasion when on a freighter he had a most harrowing experience. They were coming out of Surf Inlet with a load of concentrate ore. This had been frozen into blocks that could be handled and loaded into the forward and after holds.

It was Christmas Eve when they left, and during the night, with the warmth of the ship, the slabs of concentrate began to thaw, turning into a porridge-like mass of matter that settled to the starboard side of the hold.

By nine o'clock Christmas morning the ship had a list of forty-five degrees to starboard—lying almost flat on her side and becoming steadily worse.

The Skipper ordered his men down into the after hold to try and shift some of the material there, which had not thawed, to the port side. This was a most hazardous job, for the men felt trapped down below, and any moment the ship could roll over and take them with it.

Knowing the coast as intimately as he did, the Skipper risked running his ship aground on a tiny sand beach, barely wide enough to take her, that lay amid the rocks and boulders of Millbank Sound.

With her nose pushed into the beach, he ordered his men to take four steel lines ashore and anchor them to trees, boulders or logs. Then the niggerhead winches were started up and the ship was pulled up hard and fast into the sand with two stern lines and two bow lines holding her in position against the wind and waves.

All the men were now ordered below into the porridge-like mass of concentrate, and with a bucket brigade began to move it from one side to the other. This was achieved by digging it from the center in a trench, which was filled with planks and driftwood timber off the beach, acting as a barricade the higher they piled it on the port side.

For three days and three nights the men sweated and toiled at this work without letup. Food was hardly to be had. Since the ship listed so badly, not a pot or pan could be kept on the stove to cook a meal. What a Christmas that was!

Eventually, little by little, the weight was shifted, and finally the ship started to right herself. When the next extreme high tide came along, the shore lines were loosed, the engines were put full astern, and she backed out of her makeshift berth.

In those days, his ship had no wireless communication with shore. Naturally when she failed to show up on schedule, it was assumed she had gone to the bottom. Imagine the owner's surprise when three days later, she came steaming in out of nowhere.

It was through experiences of this sort, along with many others, that "built-in" abilities of natural resourcefulness, and instinct for survival in the "Graveyard of the Pacific" were acquired. These attributes cannot be gained in one or two seasons at sea. They require, instead, years and years of apprenticeship in some of the world's most treacherous waters.

This is not an idle statement, for there have been more men lost and ships wrecked per mile, along the coast of Vancouver Island, than perhaps any other spot in the world except Sable Island on the East Coast of the Continent.

In the early days of sailing and navigation, before there were adequate charts or proper lighthouses, the toll of ships here defies description. Even today despite all the navigational aids available, and all the warning techniques of modern science in use, a steady quota of fishing craft and steamers find their graves on this grim coast every year. From north to south as a sea gull might fly the Island is only 400 miles long. Yet because of its innumerable sounds, bays, inlets, and fiordlike channels, the actual coast line must be at least 1,000 miles in length.

This tortuous strand, studded with rocks, reefs and black headlands; whipped to frenzy by furious winds; draped in clouds, darkness, mist and dense fog; with all around the dark brooding forests under rain, has been the happy hunting ground for the Skipper with his fellow missionaries for more than twenty years. Hunting not for wealth of forest, mine or fishing —but for the wealth of human hearts which endures forever.

After having been in commerical shipping for so long, the Skipper returned to his home village on the Island for several quiet years.

One day while walking down the street in Courtenay he saw a cheerful, rough-and-ready character who appeared to fit the description of the Shantyman Missionary he had heard about— who came that way occasionally. Both men seemed instinctively drawn to each other. Though not having met, they greeted one another, and from that moment a bond of fast friendship grew which has deepened with time. In His own great faithfulness God had fitted and equipped a man who could take the burden of the boat work from the Missionary's mind.

This was a most important consideration just now, for the Second World War had just started, and the Missionary felt a very profound call to minister to the servicemen stationed on the Island. After all he himself had been a military man in his youth, and there was a natural, though God-inspired, desire to do something for those fellows and girls who flocked to the forces.

It was obvious that he could not do both this work and the boat work. As he threw himself more and more into the work of the servicemen, it was apparent that "Messenger II" would have to stand idle with no one to man her.

Once again dear old "Uncle Sammy" and his committee cast about for someone to fill this post. They were led to invite the Skipper to Victoria to see if he would consider joining their association.

The Skipper went down to discuss the prospects with them, telling a little of how his own past career perhaps fitted him for the task. Nonetheless he wished only to obey God's will in the matter.

To this end, all of those concerned gave themselves to prayer

—seeking God's guidance in the decision. Finally the Skipper felt assured that this was in fact the work God intended him to take up.

From that time on "Messenger II" came under his command.

During much of this time, when not sailing alone, he had in his company young men who were to be inspired mightily by his life and work. Some of these fellows were destined later to establish their own mission enterprises on the coast, some of which have grown into flourishing works under the providence and benediction of God's Hand.

Others who have sailed with the Skipper as engineers, deck hands, flunkies or mere fellow passengers have felt in his company the Presence of the Master. Out of this there is no doubt but that many have sensed for the first time the touch of Christ upon their shoulders, bidding them too to go out into the stormy seas of life, bent on His service.

Such men and women are to be found scattered across the globe. Nor with the years has the quiet still Voice that they heard for the first time in the wheelhouse of the Skipper's boat ever faded from their ears: "Go ye!"

Sailing a Small Boat

To most people small boats are fascinating. A man need not have brine in his beard to hanker for the thrill of feeling a deck rolling under his feet. Nor must one necessarily be a seaman to sense the sweet contentment that comes with the curl of a bow wave curving to port and starboard, while the breeze sings in the rigging.

The glint of sunshine off sparkling summer seas; the cohorts of cumulous clouds that march over the broad horizon; the smooth, soft flight of sea birds circling the boat; all of these are fragments of the bright romantic side of sailing.

There is though a dark, forbidding side as well. It is made up of overcast skies black with thunder and rain; the grasping, clinging fogs that fold their shrouds about the coast; the sudden squalls and wicked winds that stir and plow the deeps until the sea heaves angrily; the changing tides, ground swells, rocks, reefs and floating deadheads that endanger men and ships.

Added to all of this there is the eternal, ceaseless, never-ending upkeep of a craft that endures endless abuse in such stormy waters.

There is the painting, the scraping; the replacement of engine parts; the polish of metal and mending of lines.

As had been said so neatly—men always call boats by a feminine name—"Because, like a woman, they demand one's undivided attention."

Like most things in life a boat is at its best when busy and working, especially boats with wooden hulls. The entire upper structure is then drenched with salt water which keeps the timbers tight and helps to preserve the planking. If the craft stands idle too long, the woodwork dries and shrinks in the sun. Then the next stormy voyage finds the boat shipping water through the cracks and fissures in the hull and upper structure.

An idle boat too, quickly accumulates a regular garden of grass, marine growth, barnacles, worms and toradoes upon its under parts.

To offset this a spell of lying in fresh water each year does wonders in arresting and discouraging this growth accumulation.

Empty tanks too, soon become corroded and pitted under the relentless action of rust and sea air. Metal parts are fouled by electrolysis and woodwork becomes weathered with sun, wind and rain. Ropes rot in the sea air; chains and cables rust away; while bedding, books and stores gather mildew and musty odours.

The continuous care of all this gear and equipment is one of the important, though less obvious parts of anyone's life who handles a boat.

On the rugged West Coast with its rough weather, wear and tear attain appalling proportions on boats that are exposed to her seas the year around. Wood, metal and men are here subjected to testings not often equalled elsewhere.

In spite of all this the Shanty boys are not ones to turn tail in the face of danger. Their instructions are clear and simple: "Go—into the out-of-the-way places—the remote bays—the hidden coves—and bring isolated men and women God's Good News."

Under such orders their boats have been pushed into the most hazardous channels, and exposed to uncounted reefs, rocks and gales—all that men might meet Christ.

This is not done with any sense of showmanship or bravado. Rather it is the cool, clear-headed, courageous carrying out of the Master's command in the line of duty.

In every storm; in every dark night; through every fog; across reef and bar the Shanty boys rely not only on their own inherent seamanship that has become so skilled with years of service—but also on the Presence of God Himself in that situation.

Over their cabin door hangs a simple motto that reads: "Is anything too hard for the Lord?"

Because they KNOW that nothing is, they are neither ashamed nor slow to call upon Him at all times. Is He not the One who in His own great goodness and mercy to man has said: "I will never leave you, nor forsake you!" Little wonder then that these men take pride in telling of the numerous and remarkable encounters in which God again and again has proved Himself faithful on their behalf.

With the Shanty boys—God is not some benevolent being situated in the distant skies to whom one cries out in the hour of distress. To them God is ever-present in every situation of each day. Their actions, decisions and duties are carried out under the guidance of His Spirit in their hearts and minds. A more wonderful way to live, a more rewarding way to serve in the cause of Christ, is difficult to imagine.

Is it any wonder that when an Indian woman, a tough logger, a miner's wife, a lonely lightkeeper, or a fisherman's boy sees the white hull of the Shanty boat gliding through the water towards their beach, a grin creases the face, and the heart beats a little faster?

Not long after the Skipper took over "Messenger II," he was sailing from Victoria to Barkley Sound alone in September. The weather was moderate, though out to sea there stood a foreboding bank of dark, smokelike cloud which he felt sure was fog.

As he approached Pachena Point, he noticed a large Russian

freighter that had been driven aground on a reef. He pulled closer to shore, to have a better look at the wreck.

The freighter was still intact at the bow and amidships. The stern, however, had been broken and twisted by the action of the waves. Steel deck plates hung askew, swinging on a few stray rivets that still fastened them to the hulk.

To the Skipper it was a sobering sight to watch the rising waters actually take that ship apart piece by piece with the sledge hammer blows of its vicious combers.

As he passed the wreck, a mean southwesterly wind blew up from his port quarter. The sea began to make up more violently, pushed and crowded with a 35 to 40 mile per hour wind. The same blow shifted the dark fog bank, that stood out to sea, in towards the shore.

Before he knew it, visibility had dropped to zero, with a dismal blanket of clammy grey fog enfolding everything.

Fortunately he picked up Sea Bird Rocks, then found that to round Cape Beale, he would have to hold offshore with his boat wallowing in a heavy beam sea.

It was impossible to pick up the wail of the fog horn above the roar of his engines, since the wind was carrying the sound away from him.

When one realizes that his small boat had neither a fathometer or radar, it can be well imagined how difficult it would be to navigate only on the basis of running time and compass bearing.

There alone in the wheelhouse, the Skipper had not now seen land for an hour and a half. In the darkness of the fog he called on God for wisdom, help and guidance in finding the mouth of the channel.

Finally he felt the precise time had come to haul around and turn in to Barkley Sound. As he crept through the gloom, it gradually began to lift. To his great joy he found he was dead on course, and in the very center of the safe channel that led amongst the rocks. How good was God—how trustworthy!

It was during this harrowing experience that it became clear to the Skipper that out in that same storm, in that same fog, there were fishermen risking their lives too—for fish. If there were those who would dare such dangers for the sake of material gain, how much more imperative that those who were "fishers of men" should likewise brave the angry seas.

The Skipper, probably more than any of his companions, is continually aware of the dangers which surround him on his missions. Having such a wide knowledge and long familiarity with the ocean, he has cultivated a very wholesome respect for the Pacific. It is perhaps this careful, calculated wisdom that has many times saved not only his ships, but also the lives of those who have travelled with him for so many thousands of miles in such treacherous seas. He is the first to admit the inadequacy of his own ability, and the degree of his dependence on God. This is a true measure of a fine seaman.

There is perhaps no other area of human experience in which the old adage: "A little knowledge is a dangerous thing" holds more true than in the realm of seamanship.

Yet in spite of the wisdom and discretion of his years, there are times when he has found that all past experience and knowledge were of no avail in the face of an unexpected danger.

One night alone he pulled into Bamfield, and tied up near a service boat that was lying there. Some of the crew had never seen the mission boat, and asked to come aboard.

As he invited them into the cabin one of the men remarked:

"My, this place smells of gas!"

Sure enough the entire boat was full of gas fumes, though having lived in them for days, the Skipper's nostrils had become enured to the odour.

This was especially true with the engine running and the smell of gas and oil all about him. He began to search the boat and discovered that the bottom of the main gas tank was pitted with holes. Only the loose scale inside kept them from leaking freely. The gasoline was seeping out of the tanks, running down into the bilge and being carried the length of the boat.

In the cabin was a coal-burning stove that was used for heat and cooking. Why this open fire had not ignited the fumes and blown the boat to pieces was a miracle. Only God's protection had preserved both man and boat.

It was a similiar situation that set fire to a fisherman's boat not far from this very same spot. He fought the blaze unsuccessfully until forced to take to his dinghy. Fortunately the sea was calm, and there he sat, watching his ship go up like a funeral pyre, then sink into the dark depths of the Pacific. He was left with a long, lonely, sad row to land.

Sailing small boats can be both a hazardous and a happy occupation.

For the Skipper and his crew it is a comfort always to know that God is there as well. Most of all, this thought of God's Hand upon His man, is the great solace which continually the Skipper's wife must clutch to her heart.

Of all the Shantymen's wives on the coast, she perhaps sees the least of her husband from one year's end to the next. In spite of this she is a cheerful, radiant woman who bears this separation with calmness and fortitude.

The Skipper's wife is one of those strong, tireless, hard-working individuals who ever seem able to find both the time and energy to take on a job for anyone else who comes to them in trouble.

This generous spirit; this genial kindliness; this bighearted attitude of heart and mind are a tower of strength to those less able to cope with the complexities of life.

In her breezy way this wife sometimes remarks: "He's on one side of the Island and I'm on the other! That way we get along just fine!"

But beneath this cheerful fortitude lie the long watches and loneliness of months apart . . . part of the price to reach others for God.

The War Work

WITH THE ADVENT of the Second Great War, very sudden and far-reaching events took shape on the West Coast. The tread of tramping boots; the drone of fighting aircraft; the gunfire of naval ships became common sounds to a region that before had lain undisturbed under the murmur of its long winter rains and the whine of its westerly winds.

In a matter of months the highways, roads, and empty box-cars of the railroads that led to the coast were emptied of bums, hobos, and drifters. Unemployment, that grim ghost that had stalked Canada's men from coast to coast during the hungry thirties, had suddenly disappeared; in its place came the recruiting officer, the draft board and the employment agent.

Men were in uniform overnight, some of them bundled off at great speed to form the first fighting divisions of khaki that would eventually take their place at Dieppe, Sicily, Italy, and Holland. Others went into the Navy, and strange as it sounds, many of Canada's top naval men, instead of coming from the fishing fleets and coastal cutters, were raw recruits off the bald prairies: sons of wheat farmers, cattle ranchers and northern loggers. The Air Force too drew youth into its light blue uniform, not only Canada's men, but those from other Commonwealth countries as well, who came to Canada's vast open spaces and clear skies to train in their thousands under the Commonwealth Air Training Scheme.

Gone now from "The Graveyard of the Pacific" were the dismal crowds of destitute men. Places like the "Stranger's Rest" were turned over to the Services instead as centers for service personnel. Air Force bases were established on the Island from which sea patrols ranged over the Pacific. Lookout points; gun emplacements; radar stations; radio depots and such other defense installations ringed the Island.

After all, the only direct enemy attack ever made on North America during World II, apart from the fire balloons which were released in Japan and allowed to float across this continent, was when a Japanese submarine shelled Estevan Lighthouse on the Island's west coast.

Because of the potential threat from the Orient, especially when the allies' fortunes were at such a low ebb, all Japanese fishermen and their families were moved inland from the coast —again altering the complexion of the coastal population.

Canada's major Pacific naval base and training center at Esquimalt, just outside Victoria, became a hive of activity with thousands of new recruits arriving steadily. The same was true of the Air Force Bases at Patricia Bay and Comox. The Army had camps at Gordon Head, Albert Head and Nanaimo: all of them contributing to the mounting masses of men in uniform who were to become a very important part of the Island's wartime mission field.

These men on their doorstep were not ignored by the Shantymen. In fact the boys made it a point to contact the camps and isolated outposts whenever they could, in their travels. But most especially for the Missionary, who after all, had himself

Tootling in the Rain

Life

"The Skipper" Arrives—And So Do Smiles

Life

Old Friends Exchange Village Gossip

W. Phillip Keller

A Ranch Hewn from the Forest
Dept. of Recreation and Conservation, Victoria, B.C., Canada

been an army man in his youth, the call of the services came clear.

Wholeheartedly he threw himself into the work that bore the name "Soldiers', Sailors', and Airmen's Christian Association." In British Columbia, alone, this organization set up ten main bases where the spiritual needs as well as social wants of the servicemen could be met.

Amongst all the depots, so established, perhaps none came to be more widely known or better loved by the boys and girls in uniform, than the Missionary's big rambling house in Victoria.

Hundreds upon hundreds of young men and women walked in and out of its doors often enough that it became to them a home away from home!

For many of these young folk who found their faith and trust in God shaken under the shattering blast of derision from fellow servicemen, this house became a fortress in which their faith was strengthened and re-established in God. For some who trod across its threshold for the first time, perhaps in company with a companion who was a Christian, this became a trysting place with God, for there they had the claims of Christ upon their lives presented to them boldly. Others met their future mates in those halls, and more than one romance budded under the gentle benediction of the Missionary and his wife.

This man and woman poured their very souls and bodies into the lives of the young people who came to them. They became the virtual embodiment of "Mother and Dad" to scores of lonely ones. The warmth of their love; the geniality of their spirits; the depth and understanding of their spiritual succour to the services was a continuous benediction on the Island all through the years of struggle.

God saw all this and smiled. Much more, though, God Himself was in the work, and under the guidance of His Spirit, young men and women from all across Canada came to know Christ in this house as they had never known Him before.

At long last the war-weary years dragged their heavy-booted feet away to be forgotten. Civilian life was settling gently and

silently back over the scene. It was the end of 1945 and the
final details of winding up the work in the big house on Belmont
Avenue, in Victoria, were almost completed. As though it were
to be a final farewell, twenty-five servicemen and women had
been invited for New Year's dinner.

It was New Year's Eve, and the Missionary and his wife were
busy in the huge kitchen preparing the gigantic roast of beef,
along with heaps of vegetables that were to be their dinner the
next day. Suddenly a taxi drew up to the door, and the driver
strode in with an immense brown paper bag, from the top of
which protruded two colossal turkey legs.

"It's for you, sir—a surprise."

The Missionary took the bird with amazement and turned
to his wife: "Well, dear, God must be sending us some more unexpected company for dinner, since this turkey has been supplied."

Scarcely had he made the remark, when the telephone rang.
He was told that an old, rusty tramp steamer from Japan had
just dropped anchor in mid channel between James Island and
Sidney, a few miles from Victoria. To avoid paying dockage
fees the ship had anchored outside, and on board were a group
of China Inland Mission missionaries released from Japanese
prison camps in China.

Apparently arrangements had been made to entertain the
ship's crew over on James Island for New Year's. For the missionaries on board, however, nothing had been done at all.

With his usual vigor the Missionary threw himself into high
gear and contacted the local immigration authorities. After
some discussion, they agreed that if he personally would stand
guardian for the missionaries on board, it would be permissible
to take the entire group ashore next day for New Year's dinner.

Things started to fly in the big kitchen too, as more food was
prepared to feed the additional sixteen mouths; for there were
four children and twelve adults, all of whom had been behind
concentration camp walls in China for four years.

The next morning, early, the Missionary stirred up an old
Norwegian fisherman whom he knew in Sidney. They cranked

up the rusty engine of his fish boat and put-putted out to the Japanese freighter swinging at her anchor. So derelict was she that her holds had been filled with ashes, the only ballast it had been able to procure in Japan for the ocean voyage.

Imagine the unbelievable astonishment and delight of those missionaries to find themselves taken ashore for a magnificent meal in a warm, friendly Christian atmosphere. They had not another solitary possession but the clothes in which they stood. All had been lost and left behind in the atrocity of China's prison camps.

For the children there had never been such a day as this. The sight of a bird browning in the oven was enough to send them into screams of delight. Even the smooth, cool feel of an apple in their hands—little hands that had handled only grubby rice and bowls of sickly soup—was ecstasy. The sight of a table loaded with goodies was a step into the very halls of Heaven itself.

Two of the children had no father. He had been broken, shattered, and killed under a bomb that burst in the mission compound before the Japanese took over.

If the experience was a moving memorial for the missionaries, it proved almost too much for the servicemen who came to dinner. There they stood in the presence of men and women, who, as soldiers in the cause of Christ, had endured four years of terrible privation that surpassed any hardships they themselves had known in combat.

The food, mountains of it, vanished under the attack of so many hungry mouths. Slowly, surely, beneath the gentle stimulus of full stomachs, a contented home, and Christian comradeship, a sensation of rich satisfaction permeated the home.

Pushing back their chairs, the company sat enthralled as the leader of the foreign missionaries retold the agony and weariness of those war years. He told how the women had nailed their good garments between the joists under the floor, against the day of release. When freed, the clothes no longer fitted their gaunt frames, on which they hung loose and ill shapen—

part of the price of the Gospel that was to be shared with all men!

That evening it was suggested by the Shantyman Missionary that as a surprise they phone the daughter of their missionary leader, who was a nurse in the hospital in Toronto. She did not even know her folks had arrived on this continent.

"Oh, we couldn't do that!" he protested unbelievingly. "After all it's 3,000 miles away!"

"We will anyway," insisted the Shantyman happily.

He put through the call, and discovered that the daughter had suffered a brain injury; had undergone serious surgery; and was now lying as a patient in the same hospital. He requested that an extension phone be run into her room, explaining the circumstances of the case to the hospital authorities. This was done, and in the meantime he set the missionary parents, one at each of the extension lines in his home.

The ensuing scene, with both parents trying to talk at once to their girl, weeping, choked with emotion, was a scene that utterly overwhelmed the strong men in that room. They too broke down and wept openly at so touching a spectacle. Ah, the depths of human love and affection, tried in the fires of testing and long separation!

Following this the leader sat back in his chair to recount further the wondrous faithfulness of God to themselves during the terrible war years in the camp. Then he remembered a small book in his pocket and withdrawing it began to leaf through its pages. Finally he found what he was looking for.

The last night they were in China, he had gone alone to the top of a high hill overlooking Hong Kong. There on the summit was a little pagoda, with a small circular room overlooking the lights of the city spread below him. Standing on that hill he went back in his mind over the long years in China. He poured out his heart in prayer for this land and its people whom he loved.

As he prayed, he walked around the little room, absent-mindedly looking at the scribbled names on the wall. All of a sudden his attention was arrested by two Scriptures. Each was written in English; each had under it the signature of a Canadian naval seaman. These he had marked down in the little black book that rested now in his hands.

He read out the two names—they were those belonging to two of the very men who at this moment sat in the room with him.

So electric was the effect in that place the men could not contain themselves for the powerful emotions that engulfed the group. A petty officer took the Missionary aside: "We've got to do something for these folk. Do you mind if we go ahead and raise a fund?"

"Go ahead—by all means—" the Missionary agreed.

In the quiet, quick way navy men have of getting things done, a splendid sum was soon raised from those present and given to their amazed friends.

News of what had happened swept through the city. Gifts poured into the home from Christian friends all over town. One shoe man opened his shoe store and outfitted the entire group with new shoes.

What a day that had been! Such is the wonder of God's eternal goodness and grace to those whose trust is in Him. What a tremendous finale to the war effort.

Building "Messenger III"

THE YEAR 1946 was one of those epic and monumental years which stand out above their fellows in flaming figures. For the Shantymen this was a year of terrible trials and deep distress. Yet at the same time it became a year of soaring success and glorious gains under God.

With the growth of their work on the coast; the increasing numbers of personnel; the transportation of children to camps and the other innumerable demands made upon their boat, it became apparent to the Shanty boys that they needed a larger, faster craft to meet their needs.

After praying earnestly about the matter, and seeking God's will, the committee felt that steps should be taken to start work on a second boat to be called "Messenger III." This appears very remarkable when one considers that, as was so often the case with these men, there was no money on hand for such a costly enterprise. Moreover it must be remembered that this was immediately after the war when materials were difficult to find, machinery of any sort was at a premium, if available at all, and construction costs were riding that escalator known as the postwar "boom."

In spite of such formidable odds facing them, the Shanty boys were not dismayed. God who had demonstrated His power and

His provision for them in the past had not changed. He would be with them in this adventure of construction and finance just as surely as He had been in their storms at sea.

Exploratory enquiries began to be made in local shipyards as to the type of vessel they should build; approximate costs and the chances of early completion. They were fortunate to find a yard in Victoria which had just completed a splendid 42-foot troller for a Sooke fisherman. This was an unusually well-designed hull of exceptionally sturdy construction. With some modifications to the superstructure, it was felt such a boat would fit their service to perfection.

Naturally it was a great advantage to have the blueprints already drawn. Then, too, the builders would be familiar with work on a twin craft. So it was decided this was the type of boat to build.

It was just about this time that the Missionary was in Eastern Canada at the Shantymen's headquarters in Toronto. One day, just before leaving to return West, he went into a café for lunch. As he sat at his meal, two men whom he had met in the city before, walked in and spied him there alone. They joined him at his meal and very soon the conversation turned to the Vancouver Island work.

"We feel strongly, that you should know we are with you in your work, not only in prayer and intent, but also in means."

With this each man took out his chequebook and there on the spot wrote out a cheque for $2,500.00.

The sum of $5,000.00 almost stunned the Missionary, not because he did not believe God was quite capable of so moving men's hearts but because it came as such sudden and dramatic evidence of God's leading in this new venture.

He asked the men to send the money to the Island committee treasurer. For the faithful ones back there, praying, this would come as a grand encouragement. With this sum in hand, orders were given for work to commence on the hull. The prices quoted for the job had been in the neighborhood of fourteen to fifteen thousand dollars for the complete ship ready to sail, nine to ten thousand dollars for just the hull and superstructure, without fittings or engines.

It was agreed that costs of construction should be reported week by week. This was for two reasons. The first being that the Shantymen subscribe to the principle that no debts or overdrafts exceeding the usual thirty-day credit period should ever be incurred by Christians. The second reason was that during those hectic postwar years, costs of materials and labour fluctuated violently from week to week, generally in an upward direction. The upshot of this could very well be that original estimates could not be relied on.

In actual fact this is just what happened. By the time the hull alone, without any of the additional superstructure except the wheelhouse and cabin, was completed, the sum of nine to ten thousand dollars had been exceeded, using up all the funds which had come in for the project up to that time.

Seeing that the final figure might now very well exceed twenty thousand dollars, and probably go much higher, it was decided to launch the hull as was, rather than run the risk of becoming deeply indebted.

The faithful old "Messenger II" was pressed into service. She put a line on the hull and towed it up the East Coast of the Island to Nanaimo. Here "Messenger III" was berthed and the Shanty boys went ahead on her themselves, attempting to do as much as they could with the skill of their own hands and the help of interested friends.

This was a time of sore trial for the Shantymen. Yet in their toil and tears friends rallied round them to help in hammering, painting, fitting, scraping and building a boat that was destined to bring them all great glory.

The head of the local electrical firm in charge of the wiring, became so enthralled with the project that night after night he himself would go down to the dock and work late into the dark hours on the installations. His wife would come with him to make a pot of tea and lend her woman's hands wherever they would be useful.

When the ship was finally completed, this man was asked to present his bill for the electrical work.

"Bill!" he shouted, waving his arms, "I should say there will be no bill. The pleasure has been mine. My wife and I have been church members all our lives, we have sung in choirs and all that; but this is the only and first time we have discovered for ourselves the utter joy of life—real life in Christ—and serving His cause! If you wish to repay us, then allow us to go on a little cruise with you in your work for a few days."

Of course the Shanty boys were elated to have them. The "few days" ran out to eight months during which this couple served on board throughout all the mean wicked winter weather of the West Coast. Their lives and musical talents became a blessing wherever the boat went, and it was a sad day when their gay laughter and hearty singing no longer echoed in that cabin. For the lady, who was formerly poor in health, the time at sea had proved an elixir that made a stronger woman of her.

Not all of the bills for the boat could be met this way. For others hard cash simply had to be found, and in this God again proved Himself reliable.

One weekend the Missionary had been especially burdened because accounts amounting to over $2,000.00 for fittings and equipment had to be settled. He left home at 6:00 A.M. on Monday to go back up to the job on the boat without any funds on hand. That evening his wife phoned him long distance and asked if perchance he was in need of about $2,000.00, for evidently he had never mentioned the problem at home.

He replied that indeed he was. Then she told him what had transpired that day. A farmer had been out on his tractor plowing during the morning when suddenly God spoke to him: "Go into Victoria, get $2,000.00 out of the bank, and take it to the Missionary."

He immediately stopped plowing, left the field, drove into Victoria and withdrew two one-thousand-dollar Canadian National Railway savings bonds from his safety deposit box!

These he took to the Missionary's home that afternoon and

presented them to his wife with the remark: "God told me you needed this money today!"

The delight, joy and thanksgiving on that boat can be well imagined. How wonderful it is when men obey the still, small, constraining Voice of God's Spirit speaking to them as this farmer had.

The work on the boat continued to progress very well indeed. Many helping hands and faithful friends contributed to its ultimate completion, though the task took many long months.

Finally there came the installation of the engines. The craft had been designed initially for a diesel motor, but because of postwar shortages this unit was not available at the time. In its place were installed twin gasoline engines of the best design then procurable.

Although these were not recommended for more than a very few years service, under such arduous conditions, it actually transpired that they performed splendidly for thirteen years before needing to be replaced . . . in itself a remarkable record.

The last finishing touches that are put on any building project, whether it be a house, boat or machine, seem to entail expenses far out of proportion either to their size or usefulness. This was true of "Messenger III." As the months moved along prices of every part and fitting needed to complete her continued to climb to crazy levels.

Zinc, copper, lead, iron, anything metallic almost became a menace that the Shanty boys ducked from buying.

Yet, they were building a boat for some of the world's worst water, and it had to be built right, and built with the best they could get. With chins out and dogged faith in God, they kept plugging on.

It is a tradition of these men not to tell anyone of their need while they are in it. Rather they cast their care on God, knowing that He more than anyone else cares for them. Once they have had their trust in Him vindicated, and the need has been met, whether in body, spirit or estate—then they announce it to all their friends. This is that others might share in the joy and delight of God's provision in every situation of life.

It had been at the very outset of this venture in faith, that one of the committee members went home from the meeting at which it had been decided to build the boat, and there on the block calendar for that date saw this verse:

"And the LORD, He it is that doth go before thee; He will be with thee, he will not fail thee, neither forsake thee: fear not, neither be dismayed" (Deuteronomy 31:8).

On that verse, and the strength of God's promise contained in it, the boat had been built. So much a part of the project had it become that the words were inscribed on a brass plate which was set into the very timbers of the ship by the workmen. There the text has travelled ever since, a bold reminder to all that God is as good as His Word.

At last "Messenger III" was ready for the sea. From hull to wheelhouse she was spanking new and sparkling fresh. She lay at the little dock in the Inner Harbour of Victoria, just in front of the Parliament Buildings. There, in the presence of many dignitaries, with a band playing, the humble little craft was dedicated to Christ's service on "The Graveyard of the Pacific."

When she sailed out of the harbour into the sun-splashed Straits of Juan de Fuca, headed for her hunting grounds on the stormy West Coast, her food lockers were full, the fuel tanks were topped off, and not a single cent was owing anyone.

No wonder her lighthearted crew could sing: "Great is Thy faithfulness, O God my Father. . . ."

Jacko Joins the Shantymen

JACKO IS ONE of those lighthearted, witty and very nearly in-
destructible characters that are a special product of the
British Isles. The years, many though they be, which have
passed over his head, have not furrowed the brow nor dimmed
the brightness of his eyes as they would have done already with
most men twenty years his junior.

His tall rugged frame carries a surprising resilience for a
man almost eighty. This is proved by his ability to still play
several sets of tennis in a single afternoon . . . and a surprisingly
good game he plays too with his long arms and even longer legs.

It was tennis which was originally the means whereby God
actually got His Hand on this gay young fellow. Going to the
tennis courts one morning early to play with a friend, he saw a
young lady there alone waiting for a game. Jacko, not wishing
to see her miss a set, invited her to join their game. From this
simple introduction a fine companionship sprang up, which
reached its pinnacle at the point where Jacko decided to leave
England to try his fortune in Canada.

Wishing to show his regard for the girl he bought her a beautiful tennis racquet as a parting gift. She for her part, presented
Jacko with a Bible to take with him, asking that he would read
it.

"What a present!" he thought to himself. Still, Jacko did this as his ship plowed through the grey waters of the North Atlantic. The Scripture passage that gripped him beyond his escaping it, was the story of the prodigal son. In the remarkable manner whereby God's Spirit uses God's Word in the heart, this account of the prodigal seemed a perfect picture of himself, striking his conscience like a ten-ton hammer.

But he was still full of grand ideas for the future, ideas that the rugged Canadian West of 1906 was soon to shatter. Glowing letters received from a friend had led him to believe that he was going out to a superb country estate of a moneyed gentleman, where his duties would be those of a sophisticated bookkeeper.

Instead he found himself sleeping on the dirt floor of an 8' × 12' shack, built out of logs rummaged from the bush on a northern homestead. Instead of tea and crumpets at 4:00 P.M. served from fine china, he was having to survive on a monotonous diet of eggs and porridge.

This was a letdown, a disappointment and a discouragement. Jacko seemed to find solace in God's Word, even though as yet the great transformation of giving himself to God had not taken place. He seemed to identify himself with David in his distress and found great comfort in the Psalms.

From early childhood he had entertained a paralysing fear of wolves. This was because of the ferocious tales he had been told in his childhood of wolves in Russia. He had been at the homestead only two weeks, when one night his companion left him alone. As dark closed in, a pack of wolves began to howl close by in the bush. Jacko was sure he was destined for an early death, since the only weapon he had at hand was a bowie knife. His worst fears never materialized, however, no doubt partly because God had work for Jacko of which he knew not.

Steadily and irresistibly the Holy Scriptures which he continued to read in the little shack, brought him under intense conviction of his waywardness and rebellion against God. A deadly serious state of mind replaced the usual "devil-may-care" attitude.

Suddenly, one day as he was outdoors, walking across the open prairie land, he yielded his life to God and the great transformation was accomplished in his heart. For nearly two days he scarcely knew he was walking on solid ground. Like Paul, he had seen a great vision into the heavens. Immediately too there was generated within him a burning desire to witness of his joy to everyone he met.

He was very soon to discover that God's Word can produce violence in the hearts of those who spurn it, just as surely as it can provide peace to those who accept it. Some of his closest friends and relatives told him he had "bats in his belfry," and in very unmistakable language warned him to keep his religion to himself.

Jacko was not to be that easily crushed, however, for in his enthusiasm to give his life entirely to God's service, he decided to go to Bible school in Edmonton. After several years of training he was sent out as a missionary first to the southern part of Alberta, then later to the northern reaches around Lesser Slave Lake.

Those were grim, though rather gay years, spent on what was then the frontier of our Northland. Jacko had various preaching points. Sometimes he would travel thirty miles on a Sunday morning with temperatures hugging forty below zero. Digging kindling and wood from under two feet of snow, he would light a fire to warm up the church, then sit down to await his congregation, which as often as not might be only one or two persons. This was pioneer missionary endeavour that took great fortitude to endure. From preaching he went to teaching, then off to the First World War which kept him occupied long enough that by its end he had lost his enthusiasm for a prairie parish.

It was the gentle coast climate that drew him now; out to the Alberni valley on the island. It was there, that one day as he drove down the road, he saw a man in rough woodsclothes, with a pack on his back. He stopped to give him a lift and in the course of their conversation, discovered that this was the Shantyman Missionary.

A friendship sprang up between the two men at once. Perhaps it was the Missionary's ardour and enthusiasm for the cause of Christ that fanned new life into the cooling embers of Jacko's own Christian experience. Whatever the spark was that struck fire between these two, it served to keep alive the realization in Jacko's heart that his life had been given to God, nor would it ever find the true satisfaction it sought until it found it in the Master Himself and in His work.

As a poultryman on the Island Jacko had been remarkably successful in developing an outstanding strain of Barred Plymouth Rocks. His birds captured numerous prizes at agricultural fairs across the country, and their egg production surpassed three hundred eggs a year. This for a heavy breed was a splendid achievement. When he decided to quit the chicken business, his flock was taken over by the University of British Columbia for experimental purposes.

From the farm Jacko drifted into the maze of local politics that eventually succeeded in putting him at the top of the ladder in the Mayor's office. It seemed that whatever he tackled, he tackled hard and effectively, always pushing through to the ultimate success he envisaged for himself. Yet with each conquest there remained that mocking empty sense of futility which marks the experience of anyone who is not achieving God's primary purpose for their life.

It should be made quite clear that during all this time Jacko was not estranged from God. He continued to bear a bright witness to the power of God in his own life. It was simply that his time and talents, given to other efforts, had not been spent unreservedly in the cause of Christ. This disturbed his heart. Repeatedly the Shantyman Missionary encouraged him to cut loose his tangled ties with politics and launch out once more into the open seas of Christian service. After all there were so many areas of Gospel endeavour where his ability could be put to good purpose.

It was about this time that Jacko was playing tennis one day when a crippled man struggled past the courts. His tennis partner, who was not a Christian remarked: "*There* is a man who could use some religion!"

The casual remark went home to Jacko's heart like an arrow. That evening he sat down and wrote the man a letter, presenting God to him in a simple manner.

The man replied that he would be glad to have Jacko call on him at his convenience, as a friend, but that as far as he personally was concerned, "God was an awful guy," to permit so much suffering amongst mankind.

Jacko went out to the man's farm on his first free day. There he told him of the wonders of God's mercy and grace to men. In due course this visit led to a fast friendship in which Jacko came and took the man to church with him regularly. In the end not only did his new acquaintance become a wonderful Christian, but also his mother and father.

The unusual sequel to this little episode was that Jacko eventually discovered that it was the father of this crippled man, who many years before had been driving the sleigh with a wagon behind it that had saved the Missionary's life during the blizzard in Alberta. God sometimes uses very roundabout methods of reaching men.

By 1946 Jacko had had enough of his political post. Boldly, at a single stroke, he stepped out of his position, and went down to Victoria to throw himself wholeheartedly into Christian work. The old desire and dream of getting out the Gospel by any means he could, gripped him again. He was no longer a young man, though his years hung very lightly on his tall six-foot frame. He decided to start distributing Bibles, Testaments, tracts, "The Shantyman" paper and any other good literature he could get. Thus there was launched from a very simple beginning the ministry which he refers to as "Gospel by mail."

The ensuing years became very rich and rewarding for Jacko. In fact he maintains stoutly that they have been by far the best of his entire career. Not that he has lain in the lap of luxury, for he has not, as anyone knows who has been into the simple little upstairs room with its cast iron stove that he calls "home."

Shantymen

"Uncle Sammy" Beside the Keel of "Messenger III"

"Jacko" in Fine Form with a Friend

Shantymen

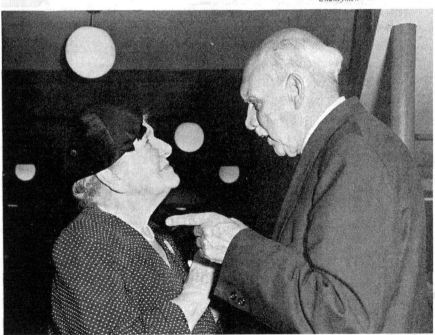

Resting in Still Waters

W. Phillip Keller

Busy Under Summer Skies

Horace Draper

But he has enjoyed the abundance of God's blessing in his own heart, which is a treasure beyond price in earthly currency.

From a simple start of sending out 300 "Shantyman" papers a month, his work has expanded until last month he sent out 900. The other pieces of literature have run into uncounted thousands upon thousands.

For a solitary individual engaged in this sort of work, he perhaps holds a unique position for worldwide coverage, since his mailing list now includes some 74 different countries. Amongst these are such remote spots as the Norfolk Islands, Tristan de Cuna, Pitcairn Island and Tierra del Fuego.

Since no one has supported him or the work he is doing, Jacko has had to look to God alone for his daily supplies. On one occasion he had the last remaining five-dollar bill in his pocket when he went to the post office to send off his papers. The cost of postage came to $4.96, leaving him four cents for himself. He boldy sent off the papers, believing God would not see him destitute. The next morning a letter from a total stranger enclosed five dollars to replace exactly what he had spent. One of his favourite little sayings is: "The barrel is empty, but praise God, it won't be empty long!"

The supply of literature to meet his needs too, is a never-ending source of wonderment to Jacko. Men and women from as far away as Florida and California, hearing of his work, have sent in Bibles, Testaments and Christian literature of assorted kinds, running into thousands upon thousands of pieces that are sent out annually.

He is ready to admit that in spite of the veritable deluge of material which he mails out, the number of men and women who have actually written to tell him of their benefit from the reading matter, remains relatively small. However he is equally quick to mention that God expects us to be "good and *faithful* servants," not necessarily as we might think "good and *successful* servants."

So it is that Jacko continues to sow his seed across the earth, leaving the fruitage in the Hands of a faithful Father.

From time to time he boards "Messenger III" for visitation

on the coast. He is a true landlubber with a marked distaste for the sea. Yet when he is along few indeed are the homes, ships or shacks which do not get their share of literature from his hands.

His persistent faithful work has no doubt done much more good than there will ever be any way of knowing or estimating.

This endeavour must be accepted as one of those services in which there is little or no glamour, very little public acclaim and certainly no prestige.

Yet, when as has happened, there comes in a letter from some little Indian girl to say she was convicted through receiving one of the papers, or perchance a prisoner makes an about-turn in life because Jacko sent him a Bible, he knows this is all terribly worthwhile in God's estimation.

In that knowledge he finds a sweet satisfaction that even a mayor's position could never afford.

The Shipwreck

THE SLEEK POWERFUL "Messenger III" very soon made her presence felt along the coast. She was a sturdy, reliable craft that plowed her way strongly through stormy seas, meeting all the demands put upon her by the Skipper. So well satisfied were the Shantymen with her performance, that they now felt the faithful old "Messenger II" could be assigned to less arduous tasks.

The upshot of all this was that "Messenger II" was turned over to the Doctor as an outright gift, for hospital work at Esperanza. It will be recalled that the hospital had lost the "Dieu Donné" after running aground in the mouth of Zeballos River. That boat was followed by the "Elizabeth," and now "Messenger II" was put into the work.

It was the fall of 1948. The doctor and his family had been up in Kyuquot Sound, holding special services at Chamiss Bay. Several attempts were made to get out of the bay and sail home to Esperanza after the meetings, but each time the seas were so rough and stormy that they had to run for cover. After the third failure it was decided to fly home to attend the hospital patients, leaving "Messenger II" anchored in Chamiss Bay.

But the Doctor's work was paralysed without the boat. He decided the following weekend he would have to fly back up to Chamiss Bay and bring "Messenger II" home. The Doctor is not a fearless man, but he is courageous, and where his patients are concerned will risk anything for them.

147

At the meeting in the little church at Ceepeecee on Friday, October 1, just prior to the date on which he had decided to leave, his fourteen-year-old son got up to his feet and declared boldly: "I believe the time has come for any man who would be saved to stand up and publicly confess Christ as Lord and Master."

This startling statement was a tremendous encouragement to the good Doctor and his wife. This lad had not been a problem boy, but certainly he was a boy with problems. Now quite obviously he had reached a major decision in yielding his will to God. In this thought the parents rejoiced greatly.

The day arrived for the Doctor to fly from Zeballos to Chamiss Bay. The boy begged to accompany him. "But, Son, we can't afford it, after all we had to buy all those tickets to fly home with last time!"

But the boy persisted. "Why, Dad, I'll pay for my own ticket, if you only will take me."

Although he felt strongly constrained to refuse the request, the kindly Doctor could not resist the lad, especially when he added: "I can cook the meals for you on the boat, when we bring her down, so you can steer and won't have to worry."

Finally the Doctor gave in, and the boy, overwhelmed with excitement, rushed off to jump into the plane beside the pilot without stopping to bid anyone good-bye.

It was early on Saturday morning, October 2, that the father and son headed out of Chamiss Bay in "Messenger II," bound for Esperanza Inlet. Storm warnings were out and some of the local fishermen cautioned against trying such a run under those conditions.

But the Doctor felt God calling him to take the boat back. He had his heart set on getting to the hospital in time for Sunday services. Already the seas had thwarted him three times. This time he would go in spite of everything.

As the little boat nosed her way down Kyuquot Sound towards the open Pacific the sea was calm, and golden autumn sunshine flooded the scene. This can be part of the treachery of the West Coast, for outside a stiff Sou'wester was picking up strength with a steady blow. By the time they got out into Boat Pass and started towards Tatchu Point, strong seas were running that made heavy going for the little "Messenger II" as she headed into them.

It was here that the engine coughed and spluttered once or twice, then began to run again.

The Doctor cut back on the throttle, easing her more gently into the wicked waves that were pitching them up and down, slowing their progress to a crawl.

By this time the boy had become violently seasick. He vomited and vomited in the desperation which only *mal de mer* can produce, until he lay prostrate on the bunk of the cabin.

With the rising wind and tempestuous waters they had only just reached the mouth of Esperanza Inlet by 5:00 P.M. Because the ocean was so turbulent the Doctor had decided to use the outer deep water channel, instead of risking the rock-strewn inner pass. This too entailed a longer run that kept them on the open sea later than would otherwise have been the case.

About 5 o'clock, just as they started to haul around and beat their way in towards the mouth of Esperanza Channel the engine stalled. The darkness of a drab fall night choked with rain, spume and menacing clouds closed in around them. There they were, a mere chip of wood flung about by the fury of the Pacific.

The Doctor went below to the cabin and found his boy on the bunk, with water washing and slopping about everywhere. He was sure water had entered his fuel lines, so he disconnected these and cleared them.

The thought came to him that unless he pumped the boat out, she might sink. With all his strength he started to pump by hand. The swish and slosh of water in the bilge carried debris back and forth that plugged the intake valve several times. Only one thing could be done if they were to stay afloat. He would have to tear up the floor boards and clear that valve. This he did, while his boy made feeble attempts to help him with the pump.

As they worked, the two men were flung violently from side

to side by the pounding action of the waves. The Doctor himself became ill and sick. In the midst of this turmoil one exceptionally huge wave struck "Messenger II" abeam, almost turning her clear over. The violent impact sent the floor boards crashing down the side of the engine room, smashing the distributor cap on the motor, and tearing the electrical wires loose from the control panel in a terrible tangle.

Now the Doctor knew the game was up. It was impossible to ever restart the engine. All they could do was entrust themselves to the mercy of God. Their dim little light continued to burn in the cabin, by a miracle. In its feeble glow the two prepared themselves for the end. Outside the wind was shrieking and gusting with wicked vengeance.

It drove spray through the portholes, lashed water over the stern and sides until everything was in a turmoil of water and foam.

The Doctor went out into this violence to put the skiff over. Scarcely had he done this when a gust of wind grabbed the oars, flung them from their sockets like match sticks, and hurled them off into the darkness. A little later with the tremendous heaving of the two craft up and down, banging and pulling apart, the rope painter parted and the dinghy vanished into the storm.

In utter desperation the Doctor then threw the anchor over. It would grab, then pull free as the boat was lifted mightily on a comber. Again it would grab, then break free, threatening to pull the boat apart, until suddenly the anchor chain snapped with the awful strain.

On and on with the driving storm they drifted. Spray hissed off the combers. Their thunder on the rock headlands could be heard above the whine of the wind. In the night they could see the ocean white, foaming, and angry and hear its roar as it broke and crashed over the reefs around them.

The Doctor knew the end was near. Taking a scrap of paper he wrote out his will on it. This together with all the money in his pockets he placed in a bottle and tied it to a leg of the table in the cabin.

He found a fairly dry life jacket and put this on his boy. Searching for a second, he could not find another that was not ruined already. His son urged him to put on one old one that was there, but he was reluctant to do so and finally discarded it.

For almost six hours the sturdy little "Messenger II" wallowed, rolled and floundered in those tremendous, mountainous seas which by now were rushing along with thirty-foot crests gnashing their white teeth upon her timbers.

Inside the cabin there was utter chaos by this time. Everything had broken loose and was flung about in a confusion of water, debris, oil and flotsam. The two men wedged themselves in the bunks and waited for the inevitable.

The boy was possessed of amazing calmness. Over and over he repeated: "Jesus, blessed Jesus; Jesus, blessed Jesus—" as though he expected full well that the Master would in a few moments welcome him home.

His thoughts too were not on himself alone, but also on his family. "Dad," he called gently, "when you get home, tell Mother I love her."

Then a few moment's silence. Again: "Dad, when you get ashore, you'll need a fire to warm you. Put some matches in a bottle, so they'll be dry when you need them."

In that strange way whereby men have premonitions of the future, it appeared then that the lad knew for certain that he himself would be lost, while his father would survive.

With a titanic crash "Messenger II" struck a rock at about 11:30 that night. The cabin light blinked out. Blackness, awful blackness was around them. This was the end.

The two men scrambled outside, not wanting to be trapped in the wreckage. They struggled to cling to the railing, knowing that therein lay a thin thread of possible survival.

The next gigantic comber picked up the boat and flung it over as though it was a bit of plank to play with. Under this violent wrenching the rail was torn from their clutching fingers. The next instant they were pitched into the cold churning seas.

"Let's stick together, Dad," the boy gasped. "Let's stick together."

These were his last words. Both of them swam and swam, trying to keep their heads above the battering masses of dark water that broke over them.

The boy disappeared momentarily, then with the next mighty wave his father was flung against him. Desperately he reached out to grasp his son's clothes, but the waves snatched him away and he was hurled off into the darkness of the foaming night.

The Doctor, though a big, raw-boned, powerful man, felt himself sinking, drowning. His lungs were bursting and in such a storm one wave after another buried him beneath masses of churning, crushing weight.

He had fully resigned himself to death. Over and over he told God that he was prepared to go Home, yet somehow he felt his work on earth was not yet completed. Now he could endure the terrible battering no more. He decided to take a last breath that would end it. Just at that very instant, an immense wave, instead of burying him, picked him up and flung him skywards. He felt rock under his feet. He grabbed it and took another breath. A second wave threw him up even higher on the rock. He inhaled again and was tossed still higher.

Like a man possessed, he began to play the waves now. Truly the power of God was present with him. Between each breaker he caught his breath and grabbed at the rock. The waves tried to tear his fingers loose from their hold. Still he clung there fiendishly, mountains of water breaking over his head, cascading off his back, clutching at his clothes.

Now for the first time he realized that had he put on the life jacket it would surely have been his death. For the surging seas around him could have caught hold of the jacket that much better and torn him loose from the rock.

There he clung, a limp, raw, beaten fragment of human flesh, but with a spirit of steel. Hour after hour the tumultuous seas surged over his weakening frame. The long slow agonising hours of the terrible night dragged slowly on from midnight toward dawn.

The words of the old hymns kept going through the Doctor's mind:

"Oh, safe to the rock that is higher than I,
My soul in its conflicts and sorrows would fly."

also:

"Rock of ages, cleft for me
Let me hide myself in Thee."

He prayed too that somehow, if God so pleased, he might the next day be able to find "Messenger II" washed up on the beach, with perhaps signs of his son's survival. He was sure that they had drifted to shore during the night, and that he had been cast up on a rock near the main coast line.

As the grey, wet, stormy dawn broke just enough for him to see, he discovered that instead of being ashore, he was out at sea, on a little pinnacle of rock that stood above the churning foam-lashed ocean around him. By the mercy of God, he had been flung upon this upthrust finger of stone jutting from the water.

When the light grew brighter he felt sure he was seeing hallucinations, for there on another ridge of rock just to the north of him, lay what looked like a fish boat. In reality it was "Messenger II." A titanic wave had lifted her up then crashed her down on this ridge of rock so violently that her keel was smashed right up into the hull. The oak ribs, like jagged fingers protruding from her sides, gripped the rock. There she lay a hulk. Nowhere was there a sign of his son.

With the dropping tide, the Doctor discovered that he could just scramble from his precarious perch across to the wreck. If he could get some blankets and a bit of rope, he would lash himself to the rock in order to last out the battering of another agonising night that was bound to come with high tide.

In the wreck he found two blankets sodden with salt water, oil and gasoline. He also got a bit of rope. Then to his astonishment he discovered his medical kit bag intact. These things he took back to the rock. While at the wreck he found two tins of canned food, their labels washed off, floating in the hull. Hoping they might just be tomatoes, which he loved, he eagerly cut them open with his surgical scissors to discover, much to his chagrin, that they both contained unsweetened pumpkin! Even in his dire extremity, he could not find the courage to eat this stuff raw.

On the way back to his rock he decided to tear a large piece of plywood off the map board of the boat, and take this with him too.

At the rock he ran the rope through the handle of his medical case and lashed it to himself. He then arranged the blankets under him to cushion the hardness of the rock. Finally he tied himself and the board above his head to the pinnacle of the reef in such a way that the impact of each wave that broke over him would be deflected.

So he sat out another grim and ghastly night with the seas pounding and surging around and over him. It should be remembered that this was October; that the weather was already cold and bleak; that the sea itself was chill and at a temperature of about 47 degrees, that this man had endured the loss of his boy, the loss of his boat and there seemed no prospects of relief in sight.

All that night he clung there, beaten, soaked and chilled. His bones and body ached with the terrible battering of the waves; his mind was weary from lack of sleep; the barnacles and rocks had cut and bruised his flesh; yet as morning broke the third day he still saw no succour.

He had endured thirty-six hours of this terrible abuse under the savage fury of the Pacific. Few men could have withstood such a trial. Monday morning, he was utterly desperate. He was cramped with cold, stiff with his bruises. Almost in a frenzy he went back to the wreck deciding to start a fire if he could. To his dismay the matches he had saved at his son's request were safety matches, not one of which would strike since the emery was gone.

At this point he prayed again, telling God that he was willing to die, but that he was confident his life's work was not yet completed. Then his song became: "Praise Him, praise Him, Jesus, my blessed Redeemer."

By this time the storm had abated. The sea became calm, and as light flooded to the far horizon he spotted a ship coming down the coast from Kyuquot Sound.

Wildly he set about rigging up a long pole with old torn sheets lashed to the top. This "totem pole" as he calls it, he began to wave like a crazy man, at the same time running back and forth by the wreck to attract attention.

The big packer "Cooperator Number Ten" headed into Esperanza Inlet and the Doctor could see men on deck studying him through their binoculars. But the ship passed on.

Momentarily he was terrified that they had not thought he was in distress. He began to shout and scream at the top of his lungs.

But they had seen him alright. They slipped into a little cove near Catala Island, dropped anchor and put a dory over the side. In a few minutes they plucked him off the rock and rowed him over to the packer.

As the men pulled him on board, and he found his feet safe on the deck, all the pent-up emotions of the long ordeal broke loose in one awful torrent. There this big strong man stood and wept unashamedly.

He had been rescued! Only at that moment did the impact strike home. Saved! Oh, precious thought!

He was of course an atrocious sight. Unshaven, dishevelled, cut and wounded; haggard from weariness; his clothes torn.

Hurriedly the cook prepared him a thumping big breakfast, while the other crew members brought out assorted shoes, pants, shirts and warm clothing for him to wear.

The packer soon had him down to the hospital. As he stumbled into the basement door of his home, there was his wife waiting with the long agony in her heart that such waiting produces.

They fell into one another's arms and wept again for their boy that was lost.

For ten days the coast was combed by the police, Indians, and the Shantymen, but not a trace of their lad was ever found.

Good in Everything

I N LOOKING BACK over this harrowing experience that befell the Doctor, most men would be inclined to expostulate: "Oh, what a tragedy, what a disaster!"

A Christian does not see life in that colour. It is the Christian's implicit confidence that there is good in everything, that no experience, whether delightful or distasteful, comes his way by chance. This is because of the simple fact that God Himself is in every circumstance of life. In other words, God is in everything that touches His children.

This is one of the great foundation stones of the Christian's faith. Looking back over the twisted, tangled trails of life, he can see how, continually, in His unfailing goodness, God has been performing His purposes for the good of His children. Knowing this, it is with joy, confidence and courage that the future can be faced with serenity, and an implicit reliance in God's utter faithfulness.

The loss of the Doctor's son and the loss of "Messenger II" were classic examples of how God could bring great good out of what might otherwise seem evil. It demonstrates that what to men might appear to be a failure, can in God's economy prove to be a splendid success.

Because of the loss of that boy, no less than five fine young men in Canadian Bible seminaries dedicated their service to

God's work in that district. One lad had died, buried beneath the dark, wild waves of "The Graveyard of the Pacific," yet that death produced five hundred-fold in a single reaping.

As for the boat, within forty-eight hours of the story breaking in the press, messages of sympathy and support poured in to the Shantymen from around the world. Funds were steadily donated with which to build a new boat costing three times as much as "Messenger II" and having twice her speed, designed especially for hospital service.

This boat was named in honour of the Doctor's son, and provided yeoman service for many years. As for the doughty Doctor, this loss only drove him the more urgently to pursue his work on the coast. He had paid a tremendous price in the cause of His crusade, so his lifework became the more precious because of its cost.

In looking over the lifework of the Doctor on the Island, several salient points should be borne in mind. The first is that he is a man unequivocally dedicated to his people. He is as interested in reaching souls as he is in reaching the sick.

His brusque, rather rough manner belies the gentle spirit beneath the tough exterior. As a doctor he is infinitely patient and considerate of those in his care.

Behind this bold man stands his wife, a fine and gracious woman. Few indeed are the women anywhere, who could have endured the hardships, the privation, the loneliness, the burden of bearing and rearing a large family the way she has.

In spite of all that the West Coast might do to break and crush her spirit, it seems only to have polished her character to a higher perfection. To be in the presence of this white-haired lady, with her pink cheeks and sparkling eyes, is to feel the benediction of a superb soul upon one's own spirit. That has always been the sensation she leaves. It is the influence of a life close to God. She is one of those unsung heroes behind the scenes.

It is entirely outside the scope of this book to recount all the history of the hospital work. At best, only a few highlights can be touched on in the narrative. Throughout the twenty-five years it has ministered to men the marvelous provision of God for every situation has been a thrilling story. Here there follow a few random cases in which the reader will rejoice to see God's Hand at work.

THE FIRST OPERATION

This took place on the initial voyage the Doctor made up the Island with the Missionary. The boat had pulled into the wet rainy harbour of Port Renfrew. The two men went ashore to the logging camp and arranged for a meeting in the bunk-house for the loggers.

After the service a young flunky came up to the Doctor and asked him if he would extract his teeth, eighteen of which were decayed.

"I never have the courage when I'm in town," he remarked. "I go to the beer parlour and get high, but by the time I reach the dentist my courage has drained away."

He was taken to the boat. The doctor got some old wire from a blacksmith shop, and with a pair of pliers, fashioned a crude face mask with a flip top. He adjusted this over the man's face, then instructed the Missionary to administer the anaesthetic. The ether was contained in a discarded ketchup bottle, with a cork that had been slit. A rag was tied over the top, and through this the ether was sprinkled on the mask.

"Keep pouring it on," the Doctor told his assistant. "Keep pouring it on."

The next moment the man began to gag, then suddenly swallowed his tongue and passed out cold. The Missionary trembled with fright, for he was sure the man had died. Instantly he raised his heart in prayer to God for help. With cool deft action, the Doctor extracted the tongue, clamped a pair of forceps on it to hold it outside the mouth, and immmediately started artificial respiration. One-two-three-four . . . one-two-three-four.

It was touch and go for a few agonising moments. The man gasped, he started to breathe again, and it was not long until the operation was well under way.

When their boat pulled away from the dock a few days later, the flunky was down to wave them off. A very crooked grin crossed his face. But in his heart and in the hearts of many others, there was a warm welcome awaiting the Shanty boat any time she called in to their port again.

OLE THE LOGGER

Ole was a hard-bitten, tough, old slab of a logger who at fifty-seven years of age had never been in a church or read a page from the Bible.

He was working near the hospital as the Christmas season approached. Lest his holiday quota of liquor should not reach him in time, he ordered it sent up on the "Maquinna" a week before Christmas.

The temptation to guzzle overcame him, and one night totally intoxicated, he stumbled down to the wharf, fell off the end of the pier and was seriously injured. The old rascal was bundled into the hospital for medical care where he remained a week.

During his stay, the Doctor and nurse had spoken to him continually about the love of God as it is in Christ. Just before he was to be discharged he walked down the hall one night with a crumpled dollar bill clutched in his hand. When he met the nurse he thrust it towards her remarking: "My, I'm so glad I came here and met all you wonderful people."

Like a shot, the nurse put a straight question back to him: "Yes, but did you meet Christ?"

It was as though a .303 bullet had hit him between the eyes. He was stunned and violently angry. He stalked back into his room fuming. He slammed the door behind him with a house-shaking crash.

At 2:30 A.M. the next morning the bell rang for the nurse. It was Ole calling her. He wanted her to pray for him. There she found him, a broken and penitent man weeping before God. Gently she introduced him to the Saviour, who alone can change men's lives.

The next morning when he came to the Doctor's office, he

was a transformed man. His face was radiant with joy, and a warm love for God had possessed his person.

GEORGE—THE HARD ROCK MINER

George was an absolute alcoholic. Such a grip did liquor have on his life that his only escape from it was to hire out on some remote mine, have the pay office hold his pay cheques, and never go to town with a pocketful of "dough."

Unfortunately for George, one sports day at the mine, he turned out to be the winner of a full quart of whisky. The old firewater soon had a grip on his burning brain, making a veritable madman of him. He withdrew all his accumulated earnings of some five hundred dollars, struck out for Zeballos, and there blew the works on a ghastly drinking binge.

By the time he was flat broke, his body was utterly dissipated, and his spirits sank to the lowest level of despair. Because he knew of nobody who really cared for him, he decided to end his life. He gathered up a sack, filled it with old rusty chains, rocks and chunks of scrap metal. This he took with him down to the dock, intending to tie the weight around his neck and cast himself into the sea.

In the midst of these preparations, a strange boat pulled into the wharf. Ashamed of himself momentarily, he dropped the sack behind the freight shed and went to see who was on the boat.

The owners said they were headed for Esperanza, and would give him a ride if he cared to go. He accepted on the spur of the moment, and went along. Not having any money, he knew it was useless to go to the hotel at Esperanza, so he stumbled over to the hospital asking if he might get a bed. The Doctor was away, so the nurse sent him up to one of the wards. When the Doctor returned, he took little time with the man, knowing that it would be a while before the alcohol had run its course and cleared itself from his system. Moreover, many of these cases were not sincere in their desire to break with their drink, and were really only looking for free bed and board.

But George was in dead earnest. A day or two later he called

Harvest from the Pacific

Men Underground

A Shack on the Shore

George Blomdahl

An Indian Village Scene

W. Phillip Keller

for the Doctor. Together they kneeled by his bed and there George committed his life to God's care. He became a sober, well-dressed respectable individual who proved he had straightened out, with the power of God in his life.

Perhaps it would be well to make it very clear at this stage that up until the time that the Provincial Government entered the hospital field, no charge was ever made for beds, room, medicines or food at this frontier hospital. All of these things were given free to the patients who came. The hospital in turn had to rely upon the goodness of God, and the generous gifts of Christian friends for its support.

THE OLD FISHERMAN

One morning an urgent message was sent to the Doctor to come and see an old man who was lying in his shack suffering excruciating pain. When he arrived, the tough old salt was rolling on the bed in agony. Tears filled his eyes and sweat stood out on his brow.

"Pain, Doctor, pain, terrible pain," he moaned.

The Doctor pulled back the covers and examined his stomach with gentle probing pressure. Everything seemed in order and he was mystified.

"Maybe it's down lower, Doctor," he moaned. "I've had a hydrocele for years!"

The Doctor threw back the covers and in an instant saw the trouble: "Man—you've got a strangulated hernia!"

"No, I haven't!" shouted the crusty old character.

"Yes, you have!" shouted the Doctor equally vehemently. "And if we don't operate right away you'll be dead."

"I won't go to the hospital," he protested.

"Well, it's up to you!" The Doctor shrugged his shoulders. "If you want to die, that's your business."

Still the old fellow refused, so the Doctor went out of the shack, saying to the woman he would be back in half an hour to see if the fisherman would change his mind. When he returned the old boy mumbled, "Guess I'll go after all."

He was promptly packed into the Doctor's boat and taken

to the hospital. Meanwhile the old fellow had insisted that another doctor he knew at one of the mines be called in on the case. This entailed further delay, which could very well be fatal.

Finally about 9:30 that night the two doctors had scrubbed up and were ready to start.

The Doctor felt sure a spinal anaesthetic was not sufficient. A complete anaesthetic could not be administered because the patient already had a severe cold as well. Finally he spoke up firmly and said: "It will have to be a local anaesthetic—and God!"

The supply of dental anaesthetic was very limited, and as they began to operate the Doctor bowed his head and prayed: "God, by Your power, demonstrate Your Presence here today!"

The man was opened up and there about eighteen inches of his intestines had already turned black. They debated on the best procedure. It was decided to replace it, repair the hydrocele and sew up the incision.

During the whole operation the old man chatted away to the doctors glibly. He said there was no pain, and in a short time he was fit as an old fiddle.

The Doctor's dependence on God made a deep imprint on the man. Seeing a Bible by the bed he began to read it. When he walked out of that hospital he was a different man, both in body and spirit.

THE INDIAN WOMAN

The day she was brought into the hospital, this Indian woman was almost bloodless from an abortion, in fact she was well nigh dead. The Doctor immediately ordered the nurses to get ready to administer a blood transfusion. It proved a most difficult task and the doctor had to cut the vein to get the blood in.

After the blood had been given, he decided to make a uterine examination. The moment the plug was removed from this organ, a veritable fountain of blood gushed out over the floor and the woman collapsed. She took a deep long sigh, threw back her head and was gone with rolling eyes. The Doctor was sure she was dead. Here was a case beyond his power. He picked up the phone and asked the main staff downstairs to pray. The Doctor and operating crew fell to prayer as well.

All this time God's Spirit had put a great burden of prayer on the Doctor's wife for this Indian woman. Over in her home, unaware of what was happening in the hospital, she kneeled in her bedroom and besought God for the woman.

Suddenly she got an assurance that the Indian woman would live. She ran over to the hospital and met a nurse on the way, coming to tell her of the Doctor's dilemma. Yet already God's Spirit had revealed to her the whole story.

Faith had won the day, however, for from that moment the Indian woman began to come round. She fully recovered and went home strong.

In spite of this experience, she has yet to yield her life utterly to God. She claims to be a Christian, yet her heart is rebellious at times.

Not all who come under the invitation of the Master respond fully to His tender care.

The Other Side of the Coin

I N NARRATING any Christian endeavour, there is a very narrow path one must tread. It lies betwixt the danger on one hand to tell only of the successful achievements, and the equally sinister temptation to draw the picture too black with its attendant dangers and difficulties.

Throughout this book there has been a very earnest attempt made to keep a balance between these two. Something has been told of the major successes in which God's Hand was so apparent. A few, too, of the hazards and heartaches of the Shantymen's work on the West Coast have been related.

It would seem appropriate, however, at this stage in the story to pause briefly in order to take a very objective view of the work. This is especially important for the benefit of any young persons who might perchance read this account, and through it feel led to offer their lives in service to the West Coast.

It is one of the tragic tendencies in modern missions to glamorize the role of the professional missionary. Even in selecting and screening young candidates for the field, it would seem that there is far too often undue emphasis put on such human attributes as personality, physical fitness, and professional qualifications. It is not that these in themselves are of minor importance—quite the reverse; but the simple fact remains that any man or woman destined to endure in the work of Christ, must first and foremost find his or her strength and motivation in Christ.

Only when the life is centered in God can the reserves, the heartbreaks, the loneliness, the tedious monotony of routine jobs which are part of every missionary's life, be met with fortitude.

Handling a boat like "Messenger III" is not just a case of standing gallantly in the wheelhouse, looking out over stormy seas, feeling a sturdy ship buck and plunge her way through turbulent tides. There happen to be dishes to do down in the galley, there are potatoes to peel, socks to darn and endless scrubbing, cleaning and painting of woodwork. None of it very romantic.

It is very easy to imagine one's self going from cottage to cottage along the beaches and bays with sunlight dancing off the waves, and the summer fragrance of the forest pungent in the air.

What though, about the long, drab, dragged-out winter months when the sun only shows its weak, sickly face far to the south once or twice a week, if that; when rain and fog and dripping brush are constant companions along the trail?

In the mind's eye it is easy to picture the Shantymen coming to the door of a strange shack to be welcomed with open arms, invited in to the cheer and warmth of a crackling fire with a teapot on the stove. But what about the times when there is only a blank stare out of a dark face in whose eyes there smoulders distrust, fear, and the suspicion that here is someone to shove religion down his or her throat?

In imagination perhaps one places himself in a hospital ward, a little church, or in children's work with the glorious and grand expectation that those he ministers to will embrace the Message of Good Cheer. Instead in reality there may not be a single response to one's efforts for months and months. A feeling of futility creeps into the conscience, and one begins to wonder if all this hardship really is worthwhile after all.

So often too, young recruits come with a fine burning enthusiasm. They see the tough godless loggers whose every third sentence is pungent with profanity. They see the moored fleets of fishermen, utterly indifferent to God. They see the sordid squalor of the Indian villages.

All this drives them to heights of concern for the cause of Christ.

Yet in time they have to discover that theirs may only be a gleaning of fragments here and there. In this discovery can lie sharp disappointment. If they last, it will be to carry on the simple Shantyman tradition of quietly visiting from home to home, person to person, winning now one, and then another.

The uninitiated too will come surging in on the scene, imagining that the whole West Coast is wide open to them. It will not be long until they find that this is a hotly disputed "fishing" ground. Vested interests deeply entrenched behind the scenes with powerful influences at work, will contest every advance they make. The liquor interests, the moneyed men, the old religious orders, the political patronage are all there in strength.

Many may think when they come to this wild and rugged strand that all that is needed is more imagination, greater programs, and their own burning personalities to lift the Coast folk out of their lethargy.

It will not be long until they themselves come under the depressing spell of this grey climate. They will learn then, too, that to live there is more than just a battle of the body, but also the spirit.

It is very easy to be "down" out there, it is just as easy to be "dull." Then little irritating things assume the proportion and scale of major issues. How one combs his hair may seem infinitely more significant to a coworker than whether or not one met the Saviour in quiet meditation that morning.

All of these counter-influences have faced the Shantymen in their enterprises. Not every project they tackled has become an unqualified success. Not every program that was launched has stayed afloat. Not every person who has joined their ranks could be considered first-class missionary material.

Irrespective of all this, God's obvious benediction has been upon the faithful ones who have kept plugging away steadily in His service.

All up and down the Island the Shanty boys are loved as few men are loved anywhere on the globe. With their quiet, persistent witness and work, like water wearing away a stone, they have won their way into the hearts and homes of countless people.

In essence, their work is fundamentally identical with the Master's earthly sojourn. They simply go along from place to place *doing good.*

It matters not what form this good may take. Perhaps it is to pluck a lonely woman off a remote lighthouse and carry her to a neighbour woman where they can talk and talk. Perhaps it is to split a pile of wood for some old pensioner hardly strong enough to swing an axe any longer. Perhaps it is to clear a patch of ground from the brambles and stumps for a frontier farmer. Perhaps it is to bring some boots, clothing, toys and candy to the children of a destitute family.

No matter what is done, or how it is done, behind each action there is only that clear, clean motive . . . the love of God. This is the center of their driving force—expressing to all men of every condition and state, the love of God for them in a real, tangible manner that they can feel, see and understand. From there, an introduction to that love as expressed in Christ is the next step in meeting the Master.

Theirs is not an attempt to make proselytes, nor to indoctrinate. Theirs is simply a desire for men and women to meet the Man of Galilee, to accept Him as their Saviour. It is the old, old concept of missionary enterprise which has proved its worth again and again across the long centuries since Christ Himself walked by the Sea of Galilee. To anyone at all, prepared to lose themselves entirely in such an unpretentious life, there are rewards far beyond the power of pen to put on paper.

Those of us who have lived close to the Shanty boys, who have observed their lives under the microscope of day-to-day contact in confined quarters, are aware of the dynamic depth of their experience.

There is something utterly contagious about their work. In spite of all the difficulties and disagreeable aspects of their lot, there hovers over them a glow and warmth which can only have as its generating source the love of God within their own hearts.

It is this, more than any other single facet of their service, which leaves an indelible imprint on the young people who work with them from summer to summer.

The number of young men and women who have served as summer workers, deck hands, nurses, teachers, engineers or evangelists with these men is considerable. In fact, far, far too many to mention here.

Yet it would be safe to say that there is not one of them but would have to confess that the Shanty boys contributed far more to their Christian careers than they ever gave in return to the Shantymen.

One of the great rewards for these men lies in the simple knowledge that all over the earth, there are Christian workers, part of whose characters and lives was deeply grounded in God on the West Coast.

One of the fundamental explanations for this lies in the simplicity of the Shantymen's work. For the most part it is stripped bare of the elaborate programming, the brilliant personalities, the complex policies which bog down so much Christian work. Rather than relying upon the techniques of men, a simple reliance is put upon the guidance of God's Spirit.

It is positively exhilarating, and at the same time very humbling, to be in the company of men so intimately acquainted with God that they expect Him to even direct them in which house to visit, what tide to take, or what stranger to speak to on the trail.

It should be obvious even to the novice Christian, that if God's Spirit is given this place of prestige in the daily walk, it follows that His benediction and fruit must result.

Two brief instances will illustrate this point. A very powerful tug was tied up in Port. A young man accompanying the Skipper was anxious to go aboard at the earliest moment.

"I feel we should wait a few minutes," the Skipper replied in his soft voice. "I don't think this is just the time to go."

They waited a few minutes. Suddenly a man in greasy coveralls came off the tug and started to walk past them. In an instant the Skipper started towards him.

"This is the man to see," he remarked, walking up to the stranger and introducing himself. It turned out the individual was the chief engineer on the tug. He took the Skipper on board, showed him and his companion through the whole ship from bow to stern. At the end of the itinerary, the Skipper was able to talk to him in a most friendly manner, leaving with him a Gospel of John which was gratefully accepted.

A small thing? Yes. But who knows where it will end? What is more, the engineer might never have been met had the Skipper hurried ahead of the Spirit's guidance.

On another occasion "Messenger III" was tied at a dock with two seine boats. The men on one of the ships were a rowdy, hostile, uncouth crowd who despised the things of God. In spite of this, the Missionary fearlessly went aboard to witness to the men and leave literature for them to read.

All that night the fishermen partied, drank, caroused and created endless commotion. Part of it no doubt was in outright derision of the Missionary who was trying to sleep on board "Messenger III."

During the night the fishermen would blow their fog horns, rev up the motors until the din was almost beyond endurance. At daybreak they pulled away from the dock and headed out to sea. Before night their ship struck a reef, foundered, and every man on board was lost.

What if the Missionary had been remiss in responding to the Spirit's guidance in interviewing the men? Imagine the agony of heart and mind their deaths would have caused him.

So it is that much of the strength of the Shantymen lies in an unshaken confidence in the faithfulness of God to guide those who are prepared to follow His directions. It saves them getting into endless hot water.

A Young Shantyman Comes Aboard

A NY ENTERPRISE that is to last for long must have inherent within it, a provision for the replacement of its older members with young personnel. In far too many Christian endeavours it is naively assumed that such matters will, somehow or other, "just take care of themselves."

The disastrous outcome of such loose thinking is that the moment the central figure or figures, about whom the work is built, are withdrawn, the whole structure more or less crumples from within.

Because the old familiar face, or the same hearty voice or those warm stirring letters no longer are there, folks assume the work has suddenly come to a stop. Interest falls off, prayer is forgotten and enthusiasm fades.

God's work is too utterly important to be mismanaged this way. Where young men have been introduced gently into the ranks, given time to understand their field, then allowed to become "accepted"—the continuity of a work can be both effective and pleasing.

With the Shantymen there have always been young "recruits in training" so to speak, among their numbers. Of these by far the greatest proportion look upon this period of service only as a training, not to ultimately become a Shantyman, but for some other field of service.

This is not to be disparaged. After all, most of these young folk render yeoman service while they are with the "boys." If they go on to wider service around the earth under God, His Name is honored. The Shantymen meanwhile are delighted to have had a part in fitting them for the job. This is as it should be. For the Shanty boys on the Island, however, the necessity for permanent young blood was a pressing question by the early 1950's. The West Coast work is some of the most demanding and exhausting to be found anywhere. Even for men of rugged constitution and character there comes a day when blood and bone will no longer respond to the command of mind and spirit.

The Missionary who had severe limitations put on his strength by complications that set in after he had fallen overboard one night, was advised to slow down. The Skipper himself, though tough as oak planking, was finding that even an "old salt" has a limit to his endurance after bucking the Pacific through so many squalls. In his dry, rib-tickling manner, he would remark: "It's about time I moved ashore and took up lighthouse keeping."

God, too, knew about all this, and what was more, knew of their concern to find those who would fill their boots, to tread trails of the Island and to handle the wheel of "Messenger III."

God had been preparing the mind and heart of a young man whose life would soon be given to this work. This lad had lived in the Alberni Valley, where his widowed mother raised him in a devout and godly manner. She herself had been interested in the "Stranger's Rest," but for a growing boy, the meetings there were not a great attraction since few of his age attended. Through this contact, however, he had become acquainted with the Shantymen.

At high school age he was sent off to the Christian boarding school at Three Hills, Alberta. It was there that God got a tremendous grip on his life. Wholeheartedly he dedicated himself to service, primarily, if possible, to the Yunnan Province of China.

This was never possible, for while he was completing the Bible training course at the Prairie Bible Institute in Three Hills, all doors to missionary endeavour in China were slammed shut.

In the meantime, the lad continued to spend his summers working on the coast, generally in sawmills, attempting to pay his way through school, and still finding time to witness for the Lord.

It is significant that even at this age, his heart was sensitive to the dealing and direction of God's Spirit. One evening near summer's end he was riding the caboose home with companions when he felt led to get off with a friend, a mile before his own stop. As the two young men walked along the tracks, he opened his heart and poured out to his companion the love of God that had been poured into his own life. He felt confident that this was the hour and day that his companion's destiny would be determined. So there on the tracks, the two knelt while he sought to lead his friend to Christ.

The summer ended. He returned to Three Hills to his studies. When he came back to the coast the following spring, he enquired after his friend: "You mean Chris?" they asked.

"Yes."

"Oh, he's not—hadn't you heard?"

"What do you mean, 'he's not'?"

"He died of a sudden attack of polio just after you left."

This to the young man was a most sobering experience. It was borne in upon his mind in most dramatic terms the absolute importance of heeding the Spirit when He spoke. How glad he was Chris had knelt with him on the tracks that day. It had been his last chance!

In subsequent summers he began to do an active work amongst the local young people of the Valley. To him it seemed quite unbelievable that so many young folk had no concept whatever of God, or of Christ's claim upon their lives, even though there were churches at hand in the town.

It was just before his final year at the Bible School that one day he encountered the Skipper for the first time. The godly character, the strong personality, the utter dedication to his duties, made a deep, lasting impression on the youth.

The next time they met, the Skipper asked him point-blank if he would care to come on board as a deck hand. He was a little taken aback with the offer and asked for several hours to think it over. Finally he returned to tell him that he thought he could not, for he was committed to the young people he had gathered in the Valley, now a fine group of about twenty-five teen-agers.

The matter was not to rest there, however, since it was not just an accident that his path had crossed the Skipper's. That final winter back at the Bible School, God laid it clearly on his heart and mind that there was a work for him to do on the West Coast with the Shantymen.

He finally submitted an application to join the Association, with the specific role of working on "Messenger III." A week after his graduation he was accepted. On June 7 of that year, he came aboard. The very next day the young man whom he replaced left on his way as a missionary to Japan. He was another of the Doctor's sons, a radiant fellow who had endeared himself beyond measure to those of the coast who met him during his years of service on the boat.

The Young Missionary had a tremendous lot to learn. After all his formal education, there now remained that practical application of such knowledge. More than this, there were all the complex workings of a boat, the equally involved details of dealing with men and women from every stratum of society; the art of living happily under a wide range of conditions in which no two days were ever identical. As he himself said: "Not even your bed was your own, you slept anywhere on anything."

Youth is eager, resilient, quick and energetic. Though he was not in environment which was in every way "natural" to him, still he began to adjust readily. What is most fortunate for him, he was willing to follow and learn the ways of the sea under the severe tutorship of the dear old Skipper.

Perhaps a more difficult demand made upon the Young Missionary was that same willingness to follow and learn from the older men in spiritual matters. He had to discover for himself the great fundamental fact that much of his success in reaping souls would be because there were others, who had already gone ahead of him with tears, sowing the seed in patience. He had to find out that fifty hundred hearts were open to welcome him, not because of what he was; but because others had opened those hearts with their love, their labour and the brightness of their winsome witness across the years.

It is a measure of the man that he learned these lessons and learned them readily. In that learning he also learned humility, without which it is impossible to please God. Because of this his ministry on the coast was to become a blessed one, as well as a most effective one.

One of the characteristics which mark him out amongst his fellows, is the determination and vigour with which he brings men and women, boys and girls to a point of decision regarding entrusting their lives to Christ. He makes no secret of the fact that though every visit to every home is an opportunity to fulfill some social service, be it only a cheering word, it is essentially much more an opportunity to introduce people to Christ as Saviour. Because of this, his faithful and energetic enthusiasm under the guidance of God's Spirit has brought lighthouse keepers, loggers, and Indians to the Master. In this his own life has been richly rewarded with a fine growth in spiritual stature.

So God in His goodness provided the Young Missionary for "The Graveyard of the Pacific."

A Bride on the Boat

THE YOUNG MISSIONARY had been active on the coast several years, when it was his lot to discover an affection growing in his heart for a Christian nurse, whose heart seemed also to respond in the same manner.

The older Missionary and his wife had a part in moulding this match. Not that it was a deliberate act of premeditation, rather it was simply that this girl who was so far from her Eastern home, had, like so many other young people, found the Missionary's home one of the friendliest places in all the world. Eventually it was in this home that the two met, for when the young and lonely-looking Young Missionary came to Victoria, that house, too, was his headquarters.

Steadily under the guidance of God's direction, their friendship and affection blossomed into true love. This was important, because it has been said that a Shantyman needs to have some unusual attributes, of which the most important is "the right kind of wife."

177

This is much more than a joke. Unless these men have standing behind them, strong-charactered women, who are prepared to endure privation, loneliness, and long separation, the work of God is bound to suffer. It would not be putting it too strongly to say that at least half the credit for what has been accomplished by the Shantymen on Vancouver Island must be attributed to the sterling qualities of the feminine half of these man-and-wife teams. These magnificent women are the ones who rarely are seen. They are the ones the public seldom remembers to praise. They are the ones with the long night watches alone. They are the ones who never stop praying for their men. They are the ones who with tears and silent heart cries say, "Good-bye—God bless," twenty times or more a year.

But for a start at least the young bridal couple were on a new adventure in this field. "Messenger III" was to be their "home." In fact they had no other living quarters until several months after their first child was born. This was a wide departure from anything else that had been attempted along this line by the Shanty boys.

The "bridal suite" consisted of a wide bunk built up forward under the wheelhouse. Here, lockers, drawers, and a catch-all were installed. Several other minor alterations were made to the main cabin as well, where the cooking, eating and entertaining were done.

Naturally it was not without certain strong misgivings that the bride ventured into this new life. Fortunately she was possessed of a calm, quiet nature, coupled with a deep spiritual strength that would see her over many rough seas; many rough situations of domestic life.

As would perhaps be common to most women, her greatest concern was to keep things clean. Once things were soiled and stained with dirt, grease and oil, which are the lifeblood of boats, how was one to wash them, and where to dry them?

She quickly found that even soiled clothes can lead to blessing in the Hands of God. By the time the first mountain of washing had accumulated, they pulled into an island, and there

W. Phillip Keller

The Making of a Mariner's Nightmare

Camp Youngsters Enjoy the Surf

W. Phillip Keller

Collecting Campers

This Could Lead to Deep Decisions

found a lonely lady who was delighted to share her washer and wringer.

From eight in the morning until five that night, the two women washed, rinsed, wrung out and hung up clothes; meanwhile scarcely letting their conversation pause a moment. Centered as it was on the things of God, this proved a time of glorious blessing, both to the lonely woman and to the bride.

When by evening that day the washing was all done, dried and ironed, there had been driven home to the young bride a great lesson. She need no longer fret over domestic problems, for even over a tub, her life could become a benediction to others.

The longer she stayed on "Messenger III," the more apparent did it become to her that this could be a most rewarding and unique life of service to the lonely women of the coast. One lighthouse they visited, the keeper's wife declared that she had not seen another woman for nearly two years!

One succession of several days in a row they called at different lights, each of which had a lonely woman with family problems. The result was that two nights in a row the young mother sat up until 2:00 A.M. talking until the strings of her tongue would fain snap. The third night, almost utterly exhausted, she was called to repeat the performance with a lonely shepherd's wife.

That night her voice had virtually worn itself out, and by midnight she literally collapsed into a strange bed. Here sleep evaded her by a tantalizing strategy in which the rancher's flock played a part. Every few minutes the ewes and lambs, which were feeding around the farmhouse, would come bleating, "baa-baa" beneath her window.

Thinking it was the children calling, she would leap out of bed, only to discover to her chagrin that it was the "woolly-backs" outside.

When the children were born, they played an important role in their parents' contacts along the coast. Hard-bitten men at their worst will somehow melt and mellow in the presence of a woman with small children, and especially when they realize that these frail ones care enough to risk such dangers just to come and pay them a visit.

There is something heartwarming about the way a tiny toddler wraps his chubby hand around the strong brown calloused fingers of a tough seaman, logger, or fisherman, and in this one innocent act opens a path straight into his heart. Men who in the face of ordinary men are themselves like rock, will become as putty before a child.

So the Young Missionary's children became beloved too amongst those to whom their parents ministered. This of course is not a situation unique to the West Coast. Many missionaries from other parts of the earth have soon discovered that a child can be the best passport into the heart of heathendom. The presence of a child proves above all else that the missionary is at least human, very much a part of the human family, and not necessarily a plaster cast saint.

Strange as it may seem, the one concern which would leap first to anyone's mind who contemplated taking small children on a boat, would be their loss overboard. This seems never to have been a problem on "Messenger III."

If the weather became boisterous, or if there was danger while tying up or setting sail, they were always instructed to sit still. These orders were obeyed implicitly, and the result was a sense of serenity on board.

During all this time the Skipper of course had to share the ship with the bridal couple, then later their family. The fact that this could be done in such confined quarters without causing undue trouble to anyone, is a signal tribute to the fine spirit of these three people.

The bride has since remarked that the obvious selflessness of the Skipper, and his continual concern for the welfare of both herself and the children, are amongst her most precious memories of those years.

"If you want to know someone, live with them, that is when one discovers whether or not they 'abide in Him,'" she would say.

After it was decided that the Young Missionary and his wife

would establish a shore home, this young woman was to experience the same lonely life that was common to the other men's wives. Their first home was in the village of Tofino. There the members of a nearby Indian community made a habit of dropping in for frequent visits, always quite unannounced.

Sometimes an Indian woman en route to hospital with T.B. or other contagious diseases, would nonchalantly announce that she had dropped in for several days and would immediately make herself at home. The crowning example of this was one dear old soul who arrived fully equipped with her own spittoon. She was an advanced tubercular case, yet she stayed in the home three days, fondled the baby, and generally felt perfectly at ease. Every once in a while she would call to the young mother and in great earnestness admonish her in this language: "Now, my dear, when I am gone, you will take a bottle of Dettol and wash off all the doorknobs. You will take Dettol and clean all the bathroom. You will take Dettol and wash all your dishes. Then you need never worry."

Then as if to punctuate her remarks with full-size exclamation marks, she would haul her spittoon out from under the couch on which she reposed her wasting form, and spit into it vehemently. This done she would push it back between her tiny brown legs and carry on her lighthearted chatter.

Unless one has lived under such a set of circumstances, alone, with tiny ones to care for, on the frontier of the West Coast, it is well-nigh impossible to imagine the strain. Yet amid these surroundings, God's faithfulness in protecting this young mother and her children was ever evident. It is only because they could be entrusted to the care of God that the father dared to leave them.

A little later it became necessary for them to move to Ucluelet. Here the house they chose to live in was located in the Japanese section of the fishing village. The nearest neighbour who could be of much assistance was a mile away along a rocky rough trail that wound its way through a tangle of stumps and timber. The immediate neighbours spoke no English, and the loneliness was intense to the point where one cringed from it.

Yet the Japanese neighbours were very kind. They brought gifts of fish and crab. The young folk carried the mail, all of which helped to break the long stretches of loneliness.

The young mother, just before making this move, had been alone long weeks endeavoring to pack, while still tending her three children. Then her husband came home to find her down ill with influenza. There was a scramble to move into these new unpromising surroundings, for soon "Messenger III" would be at sea again.

The night before he was to sail, she had been unable to sleep. She turned and tossed, feeling very sorry for herself, feeling that somehow God was letting her down by allowing so many hardships to enter her life. At daybreak she went into the children's room to tend them. As she did so she sensed another presence in the room. She turned and though she could not see him, knew the angel of the Lord stood there.

It was a brave young woman who kissed her man good-bye a few hours later. The Lord had revealed to her in very truth: "I will never leave thee, nor forsake thee."

To this day she has never ceased to draw continued strength and courage from that moment.

The Children's Camps

IT WILL BE RECALLED that the Skipper, from the time of his conversion, had a profound interest in children and the winning of their affections for Christ.

There are few youngsters indeed, who, having met the Skipper, do not soon fall under the warmth of his spirit. Few men on the coast are idolized as he is by so many children. In home after home after home, his appearance is heralded with shouts of joy, followed by flying feet racing to meet him, then small bodies throwing themselves into his arms.

In his own quiet way, he often remarks: "Yes, you surely feel your time is well spent when these rascals just want, more than anything else, to be in your company."

Because of this great, profound love for youngsters, it was natural that he would take an interest in children's camps. The first one at which he helped was located at Maple Bay. Then later the hospital at Esperanza started a children's camp on Ferrer Point.

It was to this camp that he hauled hundreds of children on board "Messenger III" from up and down the coast. At times he would have no less than twenty-four favored youngsters on board at once. This was no small responsibility, especially when having to go "outside" into the unpredictable Pacific, and run through seas which in a few hours could turn into terrible combers.

Yet in spite of the difficulties of his mission, so convinced was he that this camp work was worthwhile, he persisted in assuming these grave responsibilities for a number of years.

Just gathering up the children for a camp was in itself a major enterprise. After all, many of them came from homes that were utterly Godless, and it is not surprising that some of the parents viewed this seaborne safari as a rather foolhardy venture.

Almost a day would be needed to round up the youngsters to a central loading point, either in Quatsino Sound or Barkley Sound. Then once the crowd were on board, the problem was to bed them down, settle them for the night, and thus prepare for the long sea run of about ten hours.

Imagine youngsters as young as nine and a half, taken from home for the first time, and naturally hopelessly homesick. Little girls crying, little boys sure they are going to be sick, and none of them altogether quite positive this is such a fine idea.

Only a person with the Skipper's calm, poised understanding and temperament could handle such a crowd. Here whispering to one, there teasing another, until finally sleep overtakes the drowsy heads and quiet settles over the ship.

At about 3:00 A.M. or sooner, the lines would be loosed, the boat with its precious cargo would swing into the tide and set out for sea.

Keeping the youngsters contented while running at sea was often the task of helpers and counselors on board. For now the Skipper's undivided attention was given to handling "Messenger III."

One trip the sea began to make up very heavily. For several hours the Skipper was torn between turning and running for cover, or going on. On this occasion the children were being taken home, and he knew the parents would be most anxious if the ship did not show up. So he pressed on. Seas were coming in over the stern; children were lying sick all over the place; while he himself could do nothing but rest on the goodness of God's protection.

Once they reached the still waters of the Sound, the children quickly regained their zest and high spirits. For the Skipper, it was a great relief to deliver each child home safely.

Across the years, despite the hazards of "The Graveyard of the Pacific" hundreds of children were thus able to attend summer camps, who otherwise never could, or never would. To do this has called for careful planning, skillful seamanship, and above all, the goodness of God. In all that time not a single child has come to grief.

By the time the Young Missionary and his wife joined "Messenger III" it became quite evident to the missionaries that new strategy was needed, if they were to properly serve the growing numbers of children all up and down the West Coast who wished to attend the camp.

Because of the sea hazards "outside" they felt led of God to establish two more camp sites. The first, Camp Ross, was at Pachena Bay which would serve the southern portion of the West Coast, especially the Barkley Sound region.

The second was Camp Henderson in Quatsino Sound, to serve the northern sector of the coast. Ferrer Point camp continued to care for those along the central section of the Island.

With this arrangement, children still had to be taken by boat, but the runs could be made in the more sheltered waters of the great Sounds, and furthermore, there was no necessity to expose themselves to the danger of the open sea. Another great advantage too, was that in this way many more children could be handled during the summer season.

There are generally two, or if the numbers justify it, three age groups accommodated at the different camps each year.

The effort has become a rather important and unique feature of the Shantymen's work on the West Coast. Not only is it an effective method of reaching young folks, but also a fine way of gaining entrance to homes where otherwise the door would be slammed in the missionaries' faces.

The camp program which has come more or less under the direction of the Young Missionary and his wife, is not aimed at teaching children camping per se. Its main emphasis rather, is to have the children meet Christ individually. Once this is done, the emphasis is upon their growth and spiritual maturing into effective Christians.

The entire camp schedule, though a busy one, filled with sports, swimming and fun, makes ample provision for the youngsters to be quiet and reflect on eternal issues. No tactics are used to induce the children to reach decisions that might not be lasting. Instead every effort is made to allow God's Spirit Himself to do the work in young hearts. In some cases campers come three or four seasons before they respond to the claims of Christ. Yet generally when they do, there is nothing half-hearted about it.

It is this kind of young people who when they go home with changed attitudes, co-operative spirits, and happy hearts, make an impact with their families, friends and communities. In fact so solid has been the record of their genuine lives, that the camps have earned for themselves the respect and admiration of the communities from which the children are drawn.

Because of this their future is promising. Again it is one of those situations where if God is given first place, and allowed to direct, He will prove Himself faithful in blessing the endeavour. The camp work has deservedly enjoyed the benediction of God since its first inception. God has been most gracious, not only in supplying suitable counselors and helpers for the camp work, but also in doing a great work by His own Spirit within the hearts of the children.

The missionaries have learned it is better to wait patiently for the Holy Spirit to do His office work in young hearts, rather than rush decisions which cannot last. In this they need great wisdom to direct younger workers who come to the coast with burning zeal, hoping to have every child converted by the first weekend. To wait on God's time is not always the easiest lesson to learn in life.

The camps are tent camps. This has a great natural appeal for children, and fits beautifully into the wilderness setting. The open-air life too, is healthy and exhilarating for the youngsters.

Strict discipline is maintained in the camps under close supervision at all times. But there is also plenty of provision made for sports, games and wonderful sea bathing. Because of all this, the camps have been happy, gay occasions, scarcely marked at all by accidents, sickness or tragedy of any sort. This is no small achievement when the difficulties and dangers of conveying and transporting so many people and supplies to remote spots are considered.

The setting of the camp at Pachena Bay, known as Camp Ross in memory of a venerable pioneer missionary of the West Coast, is especially beautiful. The grounds are located on an open meadow in the lee of a fine grove of deciduous trees, that break the prevailing winds.

Nearby is the beautiful sand beach, three-quarters of a mile long, at the head of Pachena Bay, which is a sheltered inlet running two miles in from the coast.

The floor of the Bay slopes very gently with a fine, firm, sandy bottom, which makes it perfectly safe for swimming, even to tiny tots. Here the water becomes warm and delightful for swimming as it rolls in over the sand. The breakers too of the high tide, allow the children a fine thrill as they play amongst them.

God has been most gracious to the Shanty boys in permitting them to lease the land from the owners each year for their camp. Up until now, it has been possible to keep it as a quiet secluded spot where the fine handiwork of God Himself has not been marred and marked by the rough hands of man.

In such a setting, God has seen fit in His wondrous mercy, to draw many young folk to Himself, while still their affections and hearts are tender. Under the starry nights, when the campfire blazes and the breakers boom on the beach, many of these children feel God closer than they ever felt Him before. Several specific instances will demonstrate beyond doubt the fact that what takes place at these camps is concrete and lasting in the realm of God's Kingdom on earth.

THE TOMBOY

She was rough, tough and quite uncouth, as far as girls are concerned. She didn't want to go to camp under any conditions, for if she did it meant she had to play with other girls and behave like other girls.

But she came in spite of such objections for several reasons, the most important being that God wanted her there. Nothing happened, there was no change in her attitude, no alteration in her life. Then Flower came to camp as a counselor. Flower was an extraordinary counselor. She had a way with girls. She learned to love all the girls in her tent, and they loved her in return. The upshot was, the tomboy was led to Christ, just a short time before Flower went back to her post in the city of Victoria.

When she had gone, "Tomboy" went into the blues. She cried until her eyes were swollen, and her face flushed. "Oh, how I miss Flower. What will I do without her?"

No other counselor could console her, until the Young Missionary's wife took her firmly in hand: "Don't you see that there are others who also need Flower, her family, her friends, other young folk?" the nurse went on in her calm quiet voice. "So the thing for you to do is to start and live like Flower, so you too can help others."

She saw the pattern. Humbly they bowed together, and the tomboy in a most touching manner, besought God to meet her and make her like Flower.

From a "tomboy" to a "flower," that was to be her path!

THE CANOE BOY

The first time the Young Missionary's wife ever saw this lad, he was paddling his canoe, and it was loaded to the gunwhales with driftwood boards and planks that he had beachcombed and was now hauling home. The lumber was to help build the family a home on a float of cedar logs.

He and his sister had never known anything but isolation in their remote home on the coast. In fact their entire education from kindergarten through high school, had been done by correspondence.

In spite of such a background, the boy had a fine outgoing personality that had been nurtured and encouraged by his godly parents. His father, because of a serious heart condition, could do only very light work, so that most of the heavy labour fell on the boy.

He came regularly each year to camp, and matured rapidly in the grace of God. In fact his dedication to Christ was an inspiration to those who knew him, and who watched his life in the camp.

At the age of fifteen he had already led another small lad to the Lord. In this act he found great encouragement in his boldness. By the time he was sixteen, he had been appointed a junior counselor, and was capable of responsibilities normally associated with boys three or four years his senior.

So clear and so simple was his trust in God, that there never lingered a doubt in his mind but what others should feel the same.

Fearlessly he would approach adults on their boats, inviting them to attend services. Little wonder then that now he is preparing for the ministry.

The camps do just that for some young folk.

The operation of the camps is not without a certain amount of additional expense attached to them. In this too, God has proven Himself again and again to be faithful in supplying the needs that have arisen.

Some men have donated funds toward their operation, others have supplied equipment, such as tanks, pumps, pipes, a refrigerator, tools, and so forth. Occasionally a fisherman will send in some fish. The sea has even been known to wash up a carton of scrambled eggs (powdered) sufficient to serve everyone there.

The two logging companies on whose land they are situated, Macmillan and Bloedel, and Rayoneer Canada Limited, have proved most helpful and co-operative in every way. They have donated mattresses to the camps, loaned their trucks, hoses, pumps and even their cabooses, for the use of the Shanty boys. For all of this, the missionaries thank both them and God who moved in their hearts so to do.

As pointed out earlier in the chapter, for Shantymen, this is rather an unusual work, yet it has proven its merit over and over. Unless they were prepared to take on the task, hundreds of children on the lonely coast simply would never get such an opportunity. On the East Coast of the Island, and on the mainland coast there are numerous children's camps, but the cost and complications of getting West Coast children to them would make it impossible for most young folk to ever attend them. So it is that the Shanty boys look on this as part of their job, and these youngsters as their "kids" in Christ.

Some Close Calls

I T WAS WHILE SERVING the camp at Pachena Bay that perhaps the Shanty Boys came closest to losing their "darling"
—"Messenger III."

During the intervening years there had come into their
hands another craft called "Jonathan." This was a faster boat
than "Messenger III"; she drew less water and was useful for
such tasks as provisioning the camps, hauling children and general chores.

Both boats were anchored in the bay, and the Skipper made
a practice of sleeping alone on the "Jonathan" at night. There
was no one on board "Messenger III," which had ridden at
anchor lying idle for nearly a week.

One night the Skipper noticed the sound of heavy surf outside the bay. With so many years at sea he seems to sleep with
one eye and both ears open for danger signals. This running
sea was unusual and strange for there was no wind blowing.

By 4:00 A.M. he got up, disturbed for the safety of his boat,
and decided to move her into more quiet waters. He pulled the
anchor and took "Jonathan" into a quiet bight of the bay.

Sleep escaped him, and by 5:00 A.M. he decided to jump

in his skiff and row over to see if he shouldn't move "Messenger III'" as well. She had been anchored fore and aft facing out to sea.

As he rowed towards her, he looked out at the mouth of the bay, and there to his horror saw three gigantic black combers racing into the bay where they broke right in front of "Messenger III."

This was a critical situation because the tide was dropping steadily, and already there was little water left in the Bay. Between the breakers the six- to seven-foot troughs could easily crash the boat onto the sea bottom.

By rowing wildly, he himself was able to get out just in front of the breakers before they broke and so saved himself from being swamped.

In a flash he realized he would need help to move "Messenger III." Hurriedly he rowed his skiff to shore—ran it into the sand and raced over to the camp to rouse the Young Missionary. Quickly the latter threw on some clothes and together they raced back to the skiff and started to row towards "Messenger III."

As they rowed, six more tremendous waves, black and ominous as moving mountains, rolled in towards "Messenger III." The men were nearly in tears for it seemed utterly impossible that the anchored craft could survive this abuse.

As each comber lifted her heavenwards, the terrible straining anchor chain would snub her tight, pulling her nose down until it looked as though the sea would race clean over her bows.

The men rowed mightily, tears in their eyes and prayers in their hearts that God in His mercy would somehow save their ship which was fighting for her very life.

With skill and the dexterity of his years in bucking the wild West Coast, the Skipper realized that they would have to row head on into the combers and allow the waves to carry them alongside the "Messenger III" in order to board her.

Just as they were doing this dangerous manoeuvre in terrible seas, the bow anchor of the "Messenger III" snapped. At once she began to fall off into the troughs of the beam sea. Their tiny dinghy was flung against her side. The two men leaped aboard; they clutched grimly at the railing, letting the wind and waves drive the skiff ashore.

The Skipper dashed along the deck praying as he ran—"Oh, God, have these motors start!"—for it will be remembered the boat had lain idle for a week.

He raced into the wheelhouse, quickly checked his gauges and pressed the starting button. The first engine leaped into life and a moment later the second motor fired up and began to run smoothly.

The Young Shantyman meanwhile loosed the stern anchor rope, trying to take up the slack and so help haul around.

The motors took a few seconds to warm up, and as breaker after breaker crashed first against the starboard quarter, then full into the stern, the Skipper eased the stout ship back into their pounding fury. He had the wheel hard over, with the rudder set to pull the boat about into deep water.

Why the "Messenger III" never crashed onto the bottom of the bay, remains a mystery—for between each comber there were immense troughs that left scarcely any water beneath her keel.

Finally the throbbing motors took the load with increasing strength, holding the boat against the awful pounding surf. Not once did they hesitate or falter. Slowly the grand old girl hauled herself out into the heaving sea. The stern anchor was cut loose with a life buoy attached to the end of the chain where it could be retrieved later.

The Skipper took "Messenger III" across the bay and there beside "Jonathan" they broke out a new anchor and set her to ride again.

For nearly thirty hours the phenomenal weather conditions prevailed, with massive seas breaking in the bay. There was virtually no wind, yet these colossal waves kept rolling in from some unknown source far out in the Pacific. It may have been some tremendous submarine faulting or volcanic eruption of the sea floor out in the Pacific that caused the seas to act so violently.

It had been a harrowing experience, in which once more the enduring faithfulness of God was shown through His preserving power in the face of awful peril.

When the anchor was later examined it was found that the fluke which was down, had a fault in it. The anchor had snapped at this fault in the metal—exactly where the cross bar is fastened. Had it broken five minutes sooner, the "Messenger III" would most surely have been driven aground on the beach and smashed to wreckage by the savage sea.

There are few small craft that have endured as much heavy weather as this boat. For fifteen years now she has plunged, rolled and bucked her way over "The Graveyard." The Skipper contends that she has somehow had to face much more rough weather than any of the other boats under his care. Some craft just seem destined to have stormy lives; maybe she is one of them. Still today she is a tight, solid, sturdy craft that belies all the tempestuous gales which have done their best to break her apart.

Another year the Skipper had a group of workers on board "Messenger III" bound for the hospital at Esperanza. The weather forecast called for a moderate westerly breeze. With this assurance they pulled out of Sidney Inlet, south of Cape Estevan. It soon became quite clear that they were running into weather not in keeping with the forecast.

The farther the "Messenger III" got out towards Sunday Reefs, the more violent became the sea. At the best of times this can be a tempestuous bit of water for small craft. Terrible tides with cross currents race around the reefs with white caps and foaming waves surging all over the place.

The weather worsened steadily. The seas got higher and higher. The wind tore at the tops of the waves, shredding them into white foam.

For several hours the Skipper headed into these angry combers on a due westerly course, but he simply had to beat around the reefs northward if he was to get into Nootka Sound—yet he was reluctant to turn "Messenger III" into such a grim beam sea.

The Splendour of Pachena Bay
W. Phillip Keller

A Troller Comes Home

W. Phillip Keller

"Messenger III'" in Heavy Weather   *Life*

"Messenger III" in a Quiet Bay . . . Friends on Shore

Life

Finally the decision could not be put off any longer. With tongue in cheek he turned her into the troughs. The abuse she took that day is something too difficult to describe in words.

One mighty sea after another would crash against her full broadside. The top would shatter off the mountainous waves and go crashing clean over the deck and across the wheelhouse roof. One wondered if the thick glass of the portholes could endure such a battering without breaking.

"Messenger III" would scramble to the top of a mighty wave. There she would teeter on the pinnacle momentarily—then with a sudden whining, sickening shudder just fall off clear down on her side. How a small boat could continue to roll and buck her way through such stuff is difficult to understand.

Water would be pouring in over the stern, everything inside would break loose and get fired around in the cabin. Such seas can make an old man of the best mariner in a few years.

With each wave one asks himself—"Will she roll right over in this one?" or "Can she take this pounding much longer without opening up some planking?" or "How much water is going down below?" or "Will those motors keep running with such a strain on them?"

Ten or twelve hours of running under such conditions leave the man at the wheel, red-eyed with staring into flying spume and spray that slash across the wheelhouse windows. It leaves him limp with fatigue; tense with nerves that are taut; and raw from the danger of such a venture.

Just last year the Skipper and his deckhand, while running up the coast from Port Renfrew, were overhauled by a terrible storm that was blowing at gale proportions.

Visibility had dropped to zero, with teeming rain, blown spume and salt spray carried off the crests.

In such conditions they were attempting to pick up Cape Beale Lighthouse. Even in the howl of the gale it was well nigh impossible to hear the horn. This is a treacherous, mean, rocky headland with reefs stretching out half a mile to sea.

Yet in the providence of God, the gale abated just enough for the Skipper to pick up some of his cardinal points. With these as a guide, it was possible to beat a way into Bamfield and tie up after facing the savage fury of the Pacific all day.

In this same "blow" several proud ships went down to their death on the coast that day. Amid such dangers and under the eternal faithfulness of God, the "Messenger III" and her crew keep on—carrying the Gospel, comfort and succour to those who are in need on the coast. That is their mission in life!

Faith for the Day

A T THE COMMENCEMENT of this book it was pointed out that the work of the Shantymen is essentially a *faith* work. This term was explained in fairly simple language, so that any reader might follow the rest of the story in that context. By now it should be fairly obvious just how practical yet poignant such a life can be.

If a life of faith; of utter trust; of simple dependence upon God functions so efficiently in the lives of men and women who have the trials of the vicious West Coast to contend with; why can it not become practical in more of our lives?

The Senior Missionary, with over forty years of such living behind him, points out that there are three fundamental concepts to this faith. Once these are grasped, even by the most timid soul, there lies within his reach the power with God which all of us desire.

First we *must* believe that no matter what the circumstances of life are—God is in them. We must see the invisible.

Secondly we *must* believe that in these same circumstances God can do the incredible. We must believe the unbelievable.

Thirdly because of the first two, we must believe God can do the impossible for us. We must step out to do the impossible.

Oftentimes Christians are beaten before they ever start simply because they do not see God in some particular situation or difficulty—especially those of their own making.

Or secondly, though they may believe He is in every event of their lives, they nonetheless refuse to believe He can alter or remedy the trouble—especially if it is of their own making.

Because of these two points of doubt, the third point of simply stepping out to do the impossible is never even attempted.

It is for this reason that very often God uses very small things to teach us great principles. This explains why so often the small events early in a Christian's career mean so much to him. As the Missionary so often points out, "It took just as much faith to trust God for five dollars when I was a young Christian as it does to expect Him to supply five thousand dollars now."

Two far removed and widely separated events in the lives of these Shantymen will illustrate this principle to perfection.

The Young Missionary had been on the Prairies to visit his family. It was time for him to return to the coast and his mission work. He was short $4.87 to buy his ticket on the train.

Though he was with his family, and knew that this small need would be met in a moment, if he mentioned it to them, instead he chose to trust God for it. The day before his departure he bade farewell to his family and went to a nearby town to visit friends. His host and wife entertained him kindly that evening, and loaned him an alarm clock to rise at 3:00 A.M. to catch his train.

When he retired that night the money was still not in hand. He committed the matter to God, then turned out the light and crawled into bed. All natural means of finding the money now were exhausted.

Scarcely had he done this when there was a knock on the door. It was his host. In the dark he reached out his hand and pressed something into his palm. "My wife and I feel we want you to have this money. We're sorry it isn't more!"

When his host had left he switched the light on. There in his hand was a five-dollar bill. The need was met! It required as much faith as though it had been ten times as much.

When every possible avenue of provision had been closed, of which he knew—God was still faithful. The next day he rode the train to Vancouver. He only had thirteen cents in his pocket—and no meals along the way—but he enjoyed heavenly meat and drink of which those who do not so live, know nothing.

That little incident, which in itself may seem to be of insignificant merit, became to the Young Shantyman a veritable tower of strength. Why? Because he knew himself to be in the hands of a reliable God . . . in whom one's trust and confidence cannot be betrayed.

In direct contrast to this event is the very remarkable manner in which God at another critical time provided funds, on this occasion one thousand times as much, for the Shanty Boys.

When "Messenger III" was built just after the war, gasoline engines had to be installed. A diesel unit was not available because of war shortages and postwar priorities.

The original two engines, which later came to be affectionately called "Skit" and "Skat" by the Boys on board, served exceptionally well for some thirteen years. It then became obvious that a new power plant was needed.

The Shantyman Committee went into careful consultation on the matter. It was also made a subject of the most earnest prayer, since it was the desire of all concerned that only God's will be done.

A diesel unit had very distinct advantages over gasoline motors . . . even though the initial cost of purchase and installation was much higher. A diesel engine was much more reliable to run; it offered far less fire hazards on board; last but by no means least it was a much more economical proposition to operate, representing only a small portion of costs incurred by gas engines either for running or repairs.

About this time the agent for the British firm that manufactures Gardiner diesel engines met with the Committee. He had been most successful as his company's representative in the Far East, and had now been appointed to British Columbia.

Being a keen Christian he was anxious to be of service to the Shantymen and took a special interest in the project of installing a new engine in "Messenger III." Finally, after some deliberations he offered to supply the engine at cost. He himself would oversee the installation without charge. As though this was not enough, all sub-contracts would be put in at cost, without the usual ten per cent service fee.

The Senior Missionary was away in the back country at this time and could not be present at the deliberations. One thing he knew though, was that the treasury was empty and not a cent was available for a project of this sort, which even at such favourable terms, would cost in the neighborhood of seven thousand dollars, installed.

Nevertheless, so enthusiastic was everyone with the generous offer, that in their ecstasy the stern fact of an empty purse was forgotten. Accordingly an order was placed for the work to proceed, and a diesel unit to be installed.

Hearing of this the Missionary realized that God alone could now solve the situation. Here was a chance again for God to show Himself worthy of those who trust Him unflinchingly.

The very day the contract was signed, a man came to the Missionary's home. Only his wife was there at the time. He handed her an envelope with the very casual remark—"Some months ago my sister died, and before going on to Glory she requested that the enclosed cheque be given to the Shantymen." It was for five thousand dollars.

The committee were holding a business meeting in the Missionary's home that night. Not a word was said about the cheque until the discussion was over. When the Missionary's wife wheeled in the tea and cake afterwards, the envelope was placed on the cake and presented to the treasurer as a surprise.

Imagine the jubilation amongst those men, to see how God in His wondrous provision had already taken care of most of the burden, before ever the job was started.

Of such stuff is the life of faith made up. It is the most exciting, most exhilarating manner in which a man may live, irrespective of whether his need be five dollars or five thousand dollars.

Little marvel that the motto which for so many years hung over the cabin door on their boat has been such an inspiration to these men: "Is anything too hard for the Lord?"

Indeed not! Again and again they point out He is the God of the possible for with Him all things are possible.

He is the One who is ever faithful not only for material needs but every other situation of life.

He is faithful in providing funds, in providing food, shelter, clothing, every need known to man. He is faithful in protecting from harm, danger and distress those who call upon Him. He is faithful in proffering mercy, forgiveness, and His own great salvation to the souls of men.

How great Thou art—oh, my God!

Then—why don't we trust Him more?

Harmony in Homes

To the Christian Shantyman who moves from home to home in his travels, there is perhaps no more poignant ministry than that of being able to establish under God's guidance, harmony in homes, which otherwise are under stress and strain.

Our generation and age are characterized by broken homes. We live in an era when the idea of "home" does not convey that serene sense of well-being and contentment which was formerly associated with the word. Instead, there wells up before the mind's eye the thought of separated parents; drunken orgies; destitute women; bewildered children, and derelict men.

To all such, the Shantymen come with God's unchanging message of comfort, cheer, and contentment. In very truth a most important part of their work is in this area of human need. Moreover, it must be said here that because of the very nature of the people of the coast, many of them transients; because of the high rate of alcoholism; because of the rough, uncouth life of its menfolk, the percentage of such homes on the Island is high.

In this chapter several instances will be told of how God in His great mercy to men, has seen fit to restore and establish harmony in some homes. But before that is done, it should also be made clear that the Shanty Boys have seen that over and beyond this immediate restoration of satisfactory home life, there is the wider need of founding centres where Christian families could fellowship together. Places of worship were needed within whose framework young Christian lives could flourish and grow up to God's glory.

As pointed out earlier, the Shantymen's Association was not formed for this purpose. Nonetheless amongst its senior missionaries on the Island, have been men of wide vision and godly foresight. They have realized that though their own immediate terms of reference called only for the house-to-house, camp-to-camp, boat-to-boat visitation which characterizes Shantymen's work everywhere, there was a challenge above and beyond just this, which someone had to meet.

The medical work was launched this way; so was the "Stranger's Rest"; as well as the boat work; along with the children's camps. And now the outpost churches.

Once a band of believers began to meet together the Shanty Boys gave them every possible help and moral support to establish themselves as a church. They would assist in any way they could to put up a little chapel; to find a lay preacher and thus to shepherd the tiny flock until they were capable of caring for themselves.

In this manner a number of active outpost churches were established along the coast. It was a perfectly logical and sound outgrowth of the simple visitation from home to home which produced such fine results in so many lives. Every solid work has had to have some simple start with single individuals. This work was no exception.

As with so many pioneer enterprises, these halls of worship were not an end in themselves, but rather a means whereby still more men and women could be reached for Christ. This especially applied to the towns and growing communities in which they were established. For now, after so many up-and-down years, a number of these West Coast villages are indeed settling down and growing into solid towns and communities of a permanent nature that definitely deserve churches.

In the final analysis one must realise that a church is only the sum total of its individual components . . . men and women who have met God—who love Him—who worship Him. Some of their stories follow.

THE LOGGER'S FAMILY

Both the logger and his wife were hard drinkers. Many a night both parents came home so "soused" that even their children could not be cared for properly.

At last the husband walked off with his wife's purse and all her money. She needed both food and shoes for her youngsters, so that her plight was desperate. In her anger she told her husband that unless he quit the liquor she would leave him.

Then it was that one night she stumbled into a little mission and heard about the Friend of sinners. Immediately she fell in love with Christ. Not knowing how to approach a holy God, she just wept at the altar and prayed for His forgiveness.

When she arrived home, she was most unhappy, for she had expected sensations of joy to fill her being. Just then the thought struck her that if God had forgiven her, she should thank Him. So she fell on her knees in her kitchen and commenced praising God for what He had done. At once the joy of the Lord filled her heart.

Her husband came home and she tackled him about getting right with God. Nothing happened, except that he drank harder and harder, for the wedge between them was driven wider and deeper by the conviction of God's Spirit upon his heart.

Eventually even the mill boss became so disgusted with this man's drunkenness that he threatened to fire him. This was a sobering thought for a man with a wife and large family to support. He felt he too must make his peace with God, and there in the same little church where his wife met God he knelt a penitent at the altar and was transformed into a new man.

The old lusts and passions were channelled into service for God. Harmony began to come to that home.

The very first man this converted father talked to about Christ was the "pub" owner who had sold him so much liquor.

'I guess you're right!" the bartender replied. "But if I give this up—what shall I do? This is my living!"

The very next night that barman was awakened in his sleep. Rushing out of the room excitedly he ran full pelt into one of the low overhanging beams above the door. The next morning he was picked up stone dead.

So profound was the effect of this incident upon the heart of the new convert, that he pressed everyone he met to come to the Lord Jesus Christ. First his brothers came; then his sisters; his parents; his children; and soon he was preaching to crowds of his neighbours.

When a man is born again, and witnesses to the part God plays in his life, there is no telling how far the reaction will go; from the home to the uttermost parts of the earth.

THE TAXI DRIVER

A taxi driver who lived at the very end of a West Coast road, had a family of four children. His wife had found the Lord in a very positive manner in one of the little Shantymen Sunday schools. She was followed by the two eldest children, both girls, who accepted Christ and were maturing into fine young Christians.

Later a tiny baby boy came along into the family. This child was the apple of his father's eye.

In spite of the fine life of his family, the father refused to become a Christian. This in part at least could be explained by the nature of his business, which entailed bootlegging liquor for loggers and others of his tough clientele.

Finally there came a day when the visiting Shantyman Missionary was asked by the father if he would dedicate his favourite child, his son, to God.

This seemed a strange request from a man who himself was not a Christian. The Missionary turned to him and said, "How can you give your son to God, when you yourself do not belong to Him?" A twinkle came into the cab driver's eyes and in a semiserious way he replied in a broad Swedish accent, "Maybe I give my heart to God some day, too!"

At dedication service, the mother came forward with the babe in her arms to commit him to God. The father sat stolidly at the back of the rough little chapel. Before going on with the service, the Missionary looked straight at the man and asked, "Would anyone else like to come forward and give themselves to God?"

Slowly, but steadily the cab driver stood to his feet. With sure, severe deliberation he walked up to the front of the church and there stood beside his wife. She could scarcely believe her husband stood beside her now and great tears of joy filled her eyes.

The Missionary asked the man if he was in earnest about giving himself to God. He said he was and bowed his head. So the babe was presented to the Lord for His blessing, and the entire family went home with His joy uniting their hearts.

The dedication, however, was not finished. The taxi driver found that he had to give up his business because of the booze traffic. He sold out, not only the business, but also to God. After a time of struggle for himself and his family, financially, they became reestablished in a new enterprise. Now they rejoice in God's power that has become a real dynamic force in their family life.

THE TEACHER

A schoolteacher and his young wife were invited to have dinner in the Missionary's home. That evening he spoke to them seriously of Christ's claim upon their lives.

There was no response on their part and the young couple left as they had come—uninterested in the things of God.

It was some considerable time after this that the phone rang and the teacher asked if he might see the Missionary at once. The latter replied that he could arrange to meet him in his car downtown that afternoon.

The two men sat in the car and talked. There the teacher sobbed out his story to the Missionary with a broken heart.

They had had a child since they were at the Missionary's home. The teacher himself, a serious student, and anxious for promotion in his profession, had buried himself in books every night. The young mother, burdened with a baby, feeling very much neglected by her husband who was lost in his studies, began to pine for more social stimulation as a relief from her drab life.

To find this she decided to attend a dancing school and take up dancing lessons. She became a beautiful dancer and was invited to become an instructress at the school.

One thing led to another until she found herself utterly enamoured by the dancing master. Between them they had decided to go off together and she had made up her mind to simply leave her husband, home and child.

This was the terrible situation that confronted the teacher this particular afternoon, for his wife had just announced her intentions to him.

"Oh, what can I do to save my home?" he sobbed out.

"Christ alone is the answer to this!" the Missionary replied, kindly but firmly. "Both you and your wife were introduced to Him, but you spurned His offer to meet you!"

There in the car the teacher was again told the old, old story of God's unchanging love to man. There he accepted Christ as his own Redeemer and Friend.

The Missionary took him home with him. He prepared a hot drink for the man with a sedative in it to calm his anxiety, then gave him a bed in an upstairs room. Within a few minutes he was sound asleep.

The Missionary then drove over to the teacher's house. He had been told this was the day the young wife was to leave and prompt action was needed. Sure enough just as he got there she was coming out of the house, dressed like a doll, with her travelling bags all packed to go!

He invited her to get into his car and come to his home, for he wanted to talk to her. This she was reluctant to do, for she had already arranged to meet the dancing master at a rendezvous in town, from which they would leave.

"I'm afraid I can't allow this!" the Missionary said firmly. "You can phone your friend from my house and have him come to meet you there if you wish!"

This she finally agreed to do, and went over to the Missionary's house. There, sitting in the front room, the Missionary again talked to her about her responsibilities before God, and to her family.

While they were in conversation the dancing master drew up outside the house in his car and tooted loudly on his horn for her to come out.

"You just sit here quietly," the Shantyman said. "I will meet him."

He went out to the car and introduced himself. Then quietly but in a stern manner he told the man he would not allow his arrangements with the woman to go on. He then took him by the arm and invited him into the house.

The two now sitting in his front room were both very defiant and very determined that they would carry out their plans.

The Missionary in very blunt terms addressed the dancing master and told him—"You are sinning against God by committing adultery with this woman. You are sinning against society by breaking up this home."

Just at this very instant the teacher, who had been asleep all this time, was roused from his slumber by the voices downstairs.

Recognizing his wife's voice in the house he got out of bed and came down the stairs.

For a split second he stood at the front room door. Then his eyes lit on the dancing master seated across the room from him.

Like a leopard unleashed, he sprang across the room with a lithe leap. His right fist crashed into the man's left eye. The terrific blow bowled the dancer out of his chair and he crashed into a glass china cabinet in the corner. Enraged, the husband stood over him ready to kill.

But the tough, wiry Missionary was up in a flash, standing between the men.

"No you don't!" he warned the teacher. "Not in my house!" He pushed him away from the dancing master whose eye was already black and swollen. "This man is a guest in my home; you dare not touch him."

But the miracle had already happened. As her husband had lashed out at his rival, there had also leaped into the young woman's heart the sudden awareness that her husband really did love her. In that one terrific blow God had opened her eyes to see that what had happened was out of the depths of a heart full of love for her and the child.

The dancing master could scarcely move out of there fast enough. In fact he left town that very night for good. The next day when inquiries were made at the dancing school, it was learned that not only had he gone, but he had been fired.

Meanwhile back home, the man and wife were reunited. Both of them gave their hearts to God.

Their family has now increased to three beautiful children. The parents are active Christians both in their church and the community, while the teacher has been promoted to the post of vice-principal. The entire family is enjoying the favour of both God and man.

Such are the miracles God performs in His faithfulness to those who will accept and put Him first in their lives. He will bring harmony into the home, joy to the spirit, and usefulness in service to others—all for His own name's sake.

Blessed be the name of the Lord!

Under the Shadow of Death

IT HAS BEEN SAID of the men of the West Coast, that "they live with death riding on one shoulder and life on the other." The truth of this statement becomes very apparent to those who minister to such men. Logging, mining, and fishing are all hazardous occupations in which men live dangerously.

Again and again the Shantymen attempt to drive this point home to those they reach. Yet, the irony of the situation is that too often it is not until death has already struck that they are called upon to try and succour those in distress. In some instances it seems that only through death can some be sufficiently aroused to seek God.

One of the classic examples of this took place at Great Central Lake where six men, several of them important men in the logging camp, decided to go on a binge one night. They rowed across the lake in a small boat to visit the bootlegger's shack.

All night the party drank and caroused in wild abandon. At dawn they decided to return to camp, and in their befuddled condition got in the boat to row back. The fog had settled over the cold water in the darkness as though it were a drab mourning cloak.

214

SEEK YE THE LORD WHILE HE MAY BE FOUND

MESSENGER III

Life

The "Boys" Bring Some Cheer Under Grey Skies

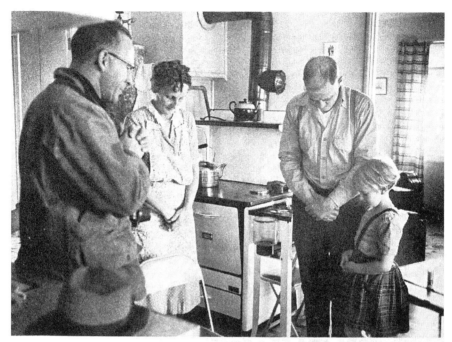

Moments of Meditation in a Humble Home

Morning Devotions in the Wheelhouse

The stern sheet of the boat had been notched to take an outboard motor. This opening was very close to the water line and as the drunken men fumbled their way through the fog, they did not notice the wavelets slopping in through the stern. Gradually the boat took more and more water with the men not paying attention to what was happening.

Suddenly it sank and all six men were in the lake.

Because it was late autumn, the water was very chill. Four of the men drowned almost at once and went to the bottom. The other two struggled to the shore and stumbled back to the camp with news of the tragedy.

Immediately there was a tremendous commotion and everyone turned out on the shore. Boats were launched and dragging operations for the bodies were got under way.

The Missionary was summoned at once by the superintendent of the camp. When he reached the lake, the fog was just starting to lift off the water under the touch of sunshine creeping over the eastern hills.

One particular woman was in great distress, for of the four men, one was her husband and the other her brother. With her the Missionary took great pains to bring comfort and solace from God's Word.

Three of the bodies were quickly recovered. The fourth was not found until the sun was well up. It could be seen lying in deep water amid a tangle of sunken logs. By dragging with lines to which hooks were attached, the clothing was finally snagged and this body was brought to the surface.

In the mass funeral service the atmosphere was still and sombre. Men who ordinarily scoffed at death and God's coming judgment, were sober and earnest. Women wept and there was ample opportunity to proclaim the call of Christ: "Come unto me, all ye that labour and are heavy laden—"

Out of this experience, through the gentle encouragement and guidance of the Shantyman, the destitute widow became a radiant Christian. She moved to a nearby town, became manager of a store and a shining witness at all times for Christ. But it took death to do it.

Another night the Shanty Boys had tied up "Messenger III" to a dock at the mouth of a fast flowing river. The boat was actually tied to the outside of two other fishing boats that were moored at the float.

The "boys" had arranged for a meeting in the village that night, and so had left the boat with only one man aboard. He was the colporteur who sometimes travelled with them to distribute his Christian literature up and down the coast.

This man was sitting in the wheelhouse going over his books and pamphlets when suddenly he heard the cry of someone shouting for help. He went outside and saw struggling in the water a man who had just been knocked off the float by a young Indian.

The colporteur raced across the two boats to which "Messenger III" was tied and onto the dock to see if he could help the drowning man. Just then the Indian dragged his antagonist out of the water.

Both Indians were desperately drunk and very violent. Fearing that there would be another tragedy the colporteur approached them and suggested that it would be wise to get off the dock.

At this the Indian flew into a rage and exploded into a declaration that he did not have to get off the dock.

"Well, if you won't let me help you off, perhaps if I get the police, they can!"

At this the Indian's utmost fury was unchained. He wheeled around and started for the colporteur. He in turn not wishing to become embroiled in a fight, fled back across the boats toward "Messenger III," hoping that the intoxicated Indian would not follow. But he did. There was just time to lock himself in the wheelhouse before the Indian charged onto the boat and tried to break in the door.

Unable to do this he picked up a heavy rope on the foredeck and with the end smashed in the window of the wheelhouse. The jagged edges were too cruel for him to crawl over to get at his man so in his frenzy he decided on another revenge.

He rushed to the stern and untied the lines, then ran up to the bow and cut the bow lines letting "Messenger III" swing out into the swift current of the river.

The colporteur realized his desperate plight now, so he ran out of the wheelhouse and threw another stern line to the next boat, catching it just before he was swung off into the current. The Indian charged after him again, across the two boats to which they were tied, and back onto the dock.

There he overtook him. He started to bludgeon him, dunking his head under water and gouging his eyes with his fingernails.

Several men up in the net loft saw what was happening. "Cut it out!" they shouted down at him. "Cut it out!"

The sudden voices frightened the Indian. He left the colporteur and fled up the path to his village. Meanwhile the colporteur, almost blinded, his eyes torn and bleeding, staggered back to the "Messenger III."

By this time word of the struggle had reached the village and the Shanty Boys, the Skipper and Jacko raced down to "Messenger III" to find their friend in a ghastly condition.

They began to try and bathe his wounds and tend his terrible eyes.

Just as they were doing this there was a bang on the door. Jacko was sure it was the drunk Indian back for further revenge. With the old fighting instinct of his youthful boxing days boiling in his British blood, he pulled himself up to his full six-foot-four-inch height, cocked a mighty fist and prepared to bust the man wide open if he charged through the door.

"Who is it?" he challenged.

"We're the brothers of the Indian who beat up the colporteur," came the answer.

The door was opened and there in the dim light stood two young Indians. They had rushed down to make amends for what their brother had done.

By this time the Missionary was back on board and he called the men into the cabin. For two hours the young men were dealt with from the Word of God and before the night was out had accepted Christ as Saviour.

The police insisted that a charge should be laid against the

Indian. This the Shanty Boys did not wish to do. Yet the law had to be upheld. The man was committed to prison and there they went to minister to him. He accepted a Gospel of John and professed to claim Christ.

As with so many Indians, his supposed conversion was not a genuine experience. He relapsed into drink again. A few months later while crossing that same treacherous river in his canoe one night, dead drunk, he upset and drowned.

Much better had it been for him to be confined to prison long enough that it could have made perfectly certain that he had indeed met God in a most realistic manner.

Death does not always come to those who are just under the influence of alcohol. It comes just as surely to sober men, to men who know their business and who take every precaution they can to save their lives. For whether men wish to face the fact or not, it remains written in God's Word that—it is appointed unto every man once to die—and after that the judgment.

The tragedy is that many godless men and women will not face this issue squarely in life. They will not make their peace with God. They feel somehow they will get by, until suddenly one day, in less time than it takes to tell it, their end comes, life is over, and all eternity faces them.

Old Anderson the logger was one of these. For thirty-five years he had made his way boldly through the mighty West Coast forests. If any man knew the logging game and how to play his cards, it was he.

It was in the days of high lead logging; the days when monster steam donkeys groaned and growled as they tightened the mighty steel cables which drew the logs up to the spar tree. This was a dangerous business for often the logs would jam behind a stump, rock, or tree; cables would snap, whiplash back, and cut a man in half.

Every choker setter had his "glory hole" or safety point to which he would leap in case of danger. On this particular day as old Anderson watched his heaving chokers, he had picked out a tremendous stump behind which to run for safety. The donkey was bellowing full blast, the logs were growling over the ground, dust and smoke filled the air.

Suddenly a heaving, churning log crashed up against a giant fir snag. The dead tree started to lean, then fall straight towards Anderson. He rushed behind his stump just as the huge snag crashed down across the stump. It splintered into two jagged fragments with the impact. One section like a gigantic fractured finger, with tons of pressure snapped over the stump to crush itself against his skull, killing him on the spot.

The Missionary was called up to bury the broken hulk of what had been a strong man's body. But no longer were there ears to hear, or a heart and soul that could respond to the gentle invitation of the Saviour—"Come unto me, all ye that labour and are heavy laden, and I will give you rest."

Probably one of the most spectacular demonstrations of sudden death occurred during the time when there was a cannery operating in Nitinat Lake.

This is a tidal lake, just as the Nitinat River which flows through it is also a tidal river. Where the lake empties into the sea through the treacherous river mouth is one of the most desperate passes on the coast.

On the one side is a dark dangerous reef and on the other a gravel bar which projects out into the pass towards the reef. To navigate this narrow channel requires skilled seamanship, even by the most experienced mariners.

If a ship should run aground on this bar, the following seas from the open ocean would immediately roll her over and smash her to wreckage.

It was Christmas Eve and the men at the cannery were going on holiday. Rather than tramp the long tedious trail along the coast, they decided to go out to Victoria by sea. A large seine boat with thirteen men on board set out from the lake, down the river towards the open ocean.

As they came to the river mouth, they ran aground on the gravel bar. The next instant a mighty wave came in and rolled the ship over, trapping the men beneath her. Of the thirteen on board, only the cook, who could not swim, survived. The other twelve men, all strong swimmers and expert seamen, perished at once.

These were all ungodly men. It was a sobering experience to those up and down the coast who knew them and heard of the disaster.

It was, if anything, a stern reminder that "God's Spirit will not always strive with men!"

In the face of such dangers, with death always hovering nearby, the Shantymen go steadily on their rounds, warning folks of that which lies ahead. Always theirs is a message of God's love to man, of His own eternal faithfulness in ever seeking to draw mortals to Himself.

With the "Shanty Boys"

THE SHANTYMEN are engaged in the most deadly serious business in all the world: that of bringing human beings into a proper relationship with God. They have to live hazardous lives on the "Graveyard of the Pacific"—for this is some of the world's most dangerous water. They are continually in contact with rough, hard, uncouth characters, for our West Coast loggers and fishermen are notorious for their toughness.

In the face of all this it would be a most serious mistake to leave in the reader's mind an impression that these Shanty Boys were sombre, sad-faced individuals who found their lot in life a drab ordeal.

Quite the contrary is true. Few men anywhere are as cheerful, as good-natured, as genuinely greathearted as these fellows. This will be endorsed hundreds of times over by men and women who have lived and worked with them on the coast.

Nor would it be fair to leave the impression that the coast Shantymen have any monopoly on these attributes. All Shanty Boys bear this same stamp upon their characters. It is the deep imprint made upon the life by the indwelling Christ.

These rugged, hardy missionaries are made of stern stuff. They have to be to meet the tough conditions of their field. Yet with their strong characters there is interwoven the tenderness, the love, the compassion which has its spring in God Himself.

In order, therefore, to give as accurate a picture as possible of these men in their daily lives, I have included this personal account of the last trip I made with the Skipper and the Senior Missionary on "Messenger III."

At the very outset let me remind the reader that both the men we are sailing with are now over sixty years of age. These are not young fledglings just new out of the nest. The Missionary has been in this work on the coast for over thirty years, and the Skipper over twenty years. Yes, between them they represent over half a century of service to these coastal men and women.

The ship we are sailing in is a veteran herself with fifteen years of pushing and plowing her way through the stormy waters of the Pacific.

In spite of all these years behind them, none of this trio show their age. The "Messenger III" is sparkling, clean, and trim. Her planking is sound, her timbers are tight, and the new diesel motor purrs contentedly.

The Missionary's face is radiant with the deep, sweet satisfaction of a full life, lived out generously for others in the service of his Master. He is not quite as quick as he used to be, for serious injuries have taken their toll of vigour; still he is full of fun, enthusiasm, and the relentless energy to tackle any job. He can still handle the lines deftly and stand a long watch at the wheel. The galley in his castle, and out of its simple appointments he produces dishes that would tickle the palate of the most fastidious gourmet.

The Skipper's face has scarcely changed a whit with the years. It has upon it the calm, rugged strength of quiet repose which is the heritage of those who walk close to God. Long staring out to sea, staring through fog and sleet and storms, has left little lines of fatigue around those clear blue eyes—eyes that are so friendly and full of fun. The body has taken its beating on the boat, but still it is erect and firm; still able to face the fury of the sea at its worst.

Together these men are like twins—not in appearance—not in manner—but in their perfect teamwork. I have seldom met a more compatible or complementary pair. Between them there lies a bond of affection and mutual admiration that transcends common friendship. They are literally brothers—brothers in the most meaningful sense.

Any time that I am with these two men together I gain the impression that "just being together" is for them one of the grandest things in all the world.

They both can be deadly serious and absolutely earnest when the occasion calls for it. On the other hand they can be as carefree, gay, and lighthearted as two boys playing hookey on a warm spring afternoon.

Day and night one hears snatches of song; gay melodies and ripples of laughter coming across the water from "Messenger III." It is the very finest advertisement possible to draw folks to God. For no one can be long in the company of these men without catching the contagion of their buoyant spirits and happy hearts.

Because of their long and close association with the sea the Shanty Boys have automatically and naturally developed a lingo and vocabulary peculiar to their own lives and marine experiences. To a stranger coming on board for the first time, such statements as the following are a little baffling:

"The belt came off the boiler and we began to sink."

"It must have been something I et."

"One more crust and I shall bust."

"Carry I out, but don't bend I."

"Devour the oysters, before they devour you."

"We're the best bartenders on the coast."

"Let's go ashore and take up lighthouse keeping."

"What about a mess of 'muggup'?"

These all reflect the rough and hearty life of these men amid boats, loggers, rough seas, and backwoods people. As one man remarked after meeting the Shanty Boys for the first time—"I always had a rather dim impression of missionaries—as though they were gaunt and grim. After meeting you fellows I have a very different idea." It may well have been an impression that finally induced him to entrust his life to the Lord.

So it was with these two men that I set out for another week at sea; just to make the usual calls, the ordinary rounds of isolated homes which are their field.

"Messenger III," gleaming white, with her neat black trim, was tied to the float at the end of a long, long dock that ran out into the channel. We packed cartons of food, boxes of clothes and bundles of literature down the dock to the ship. Because the tide was very low, almost zero, it was a steep descent down the stairs at the end of the dock. The Skipper's little golden-haired granddaughter kept racing up and down the dock, helping to hold parcels, and saving steps for the older ones.

By the time everything was stowed, and the engine room checked, a calm, cold winter night had settled across the bay.

Most men would have called it a day. But not these Shantymen. Total darkness blanketed the water now and long lean fingers of light reached out across the sea from homes along the shore. The Skipper started the motor and let her idle to warm up. We checked our port and starboard travelling lights— loosed the lines then slipped smoothly into the channel.

Over everything there hung that calm, still, mysterious mood that pervades any parting at sea by dark. I stood on the deck and watched the white wash of the bow wave grow in grandeur as we gathered speed. The deep-throated exhaust from the stack rumbled overhead . . . a steady song came from the driving diesel that was turning the screw at the stern. There behind us the water was churned into a glowing mass of white froth, dappled with lights of phosphorescence, that marked our path across the dark velvet of the sea.

Up in the wheelhouse I could hear the Skipper crooning to himself in his deep, deep voice—"There's a Balm in Gilead—to make the wounded spirit whole!"

From down in the galley, aft, there came the merry whistle of the Missionary as he rustled around in the cabin, stowing things away, getting shipshape for sea.

Overhead I could see no stars. A high fog hung above us, casting a weird glow from the light reflected off the water.

I slipped into the wheelhouse. The Skipper was still crooning to himself. He had taken a compass bearing and was running on course.

The two of us stood quietly in the darkened wheelhouse—no noise—no commotion—just the throb of the ship under our feet, and the soft crooning of a man in love with his work.

Presently we picked up a beacon light on the far side of the dark channel down which we were running. Then beyond that another blinker light.

"That's the one I'm looking for," the Skipper remarked casually. "There's an old dock just off to the port side there where we can tie up, for the night."

The dock was soon picked up in the beam of our spotlight. Instead of being a shelter it was a shambles. Winter storms had smashed it to pieces.

We slid to a gentle stop, surveying the wrecked piling and broken floats.

Gently the skipper backed out and we found a large ferry at another mooring close by. There we tied alongside for the night.

"There's a family on this Island I want to visit," the Skipper said softly. "They have two boys who should go to camp next summer."

So we slipped into heavy wool jackets and went ashore. The sea air was damp and drilling. I was glad we had a brisk hike up the little gravel road that wound its way from the beach to the home on the hill.

Overhead the fir trees of the forest formed an arch of blackness that was dripping with the accumulation of fog and mist that moved through the branches.

A dog barked on our left from a lonely farmhouse. "That reminds me!" the Skipper put in as we tramped along. "We should have brought several sacks to get some turnips for that poor family on the next island."

We pushed on up the hill and saw a dim light flickering through the trees. This was the place. The Skipper slipped around to the kitchen door and knocked. It was flung open and there, silhouetted against the golden lamplight, was a moose of a man.

"Why, Skipper!" he exclaimed—stretching out a huge hand. "Come on in—it's good to see you!" Soon all three of us were sitting in the big rangy kitchen of this ex-fur trader from the Arctic.

Before we left that night, the man and his wife had shown us their collection of Indian artifacts which had been gathered in the far north; they showed us the polished stones and home-made jewellery which were the man's winter hobby; they showed us the elegant pottery fashioned from local clays . . . his wife's pet pastime.

Then there was the return to the kitchen for a cup of coffee, cake, and friendly chatter, which the Missionary skillfully directed around to the things of God.

Our host's two boys were in bed by now, for it was very late, but that was better, in a way, for it was easier to talk to the parents about their problems and what could be done to solve them.

Finally it was time to say farewell. A passage of Scripture was read and the Shantyman, in that delightfully heartwarming way of his, entrusted this dear family and their perplexities to the tender care of a loving Heavenly Father.   `

It was almost hard to get away from those folks. The unexpected visit; the deep interest shown in their interests; the counseling for the family; the sincerity of the men had bound steel hoops of friendship around that home that night.

It was after midnight when we tramped under the trees again

—back to the boat. As we walked through the darkness we sang. How could one help but sing? This was living the way Christ had lived.

Though it was so late when we retired, the men were up early for their devotions. This was their strength for the day. Long before daylight ever creased the eastern horizon, they had meditated long in God's Word—feeding on food from above —that would fortify them for whatever the day held.

After breakfast we had combined prayers. On "Messenger III" there is an immense book of ancient vintage. In it there is a Scripture reading with an exposition of the passage, and a prayer for each day in the year. It is written in language seldom heard in this century. It is couched in terms of delicate beauty and rare grace. No one who reads it can help but be inspired by it. In fact for me it became one of the highlights of the entire day to share in the reading of that volume. There is a depth and profoundness to its pages seldom heard even from our finest pulpits today. So these Shantymen are not short of deeper teaching.

A heavy coast fog had settled over the sea during the night. Outside everything was intensely still. Even the huge Douglas firs on the shore, a few yards away, could only be made out as grotesque monsters, looming darkly through the gloom.

"Well, we've got to go!" the Skipper announced merrily as he strode up to the wheelhouse—"pea soup, or no pea soup!"

We drifted out into the channel, and started to grope our way up the pass. We were headed towards a tiny island of rock where a lightkeeper and his family were to be visited. It would be a two-hour run and in this fog that was plenty long enough.

We were travelling at reduced speed now, enveloped in misty wet blankets of fog that curled and swirled over the ship. "Messenger III" has neither a radar set nor fathometer for travelling under hazardous conditions. We were going on dead reckoning, and while the Skipper handled the wheel, the Missionary and I stood watch on the foredeck—peering into the fog.

Because it was a dead calm day, the surface of the sea was like oil. Sound, too, carried well and before long we could detect the muffled blare of the foghorn on the rock. Slowly we made towards the lighthouse, when suddenly an immense dark shape loomed up out of the greyness ahead.

For a moment it looked like the rock. Then we saw it was the lighthouse tender anchored in mid channel.

We hove to port side to miss her, and before we knew what happened there appeared overhead what looked like tree limbs. There was a shout from the Missionary: "Rocks below—hard astern!" The Skipper threw "Messenger III" into reverse, and the old girl slid to a squatting halt on her tail. It was not a moment too soon. Because of the extreme low tide we only had a few feet of water under our keel.

Gingerly we moved back a bit and dropped anchor. Dead ahead the rock was barely visible, with the lighthouse perched on its crest.

The skiff was put over, and soon the three of us were rowing toward the rock.

Our voices had carried across the water, and when we pulled in to the makeshift float the lightkeeper and his children were down there to catch the skiff and shout greetings to the Shantymen.

We were glad it was calm, for in a stiff Sou'easter, this would be an impossible place to land.

The lightkeeper was busy moving equipment from one building to another. Before he knew what had happened, the Missionary too had slipped off his jacket and was packing loads with him up the hill.

In the house the lonely woman was talking her head off to the Skipper, asking for all the latest news from the other lightkeepers' wives he had seen recently in his travels around the Island. The Skipper for his part, already had his arms full with one baby, while two other children each did their best to crawl up on a knee; just to be near him, and listen to his hearty chuckle.

Before long there would be a story for the children. For the parents there were papers and magazines to read. Oh, yes, and in his pocket a toy or two had been tucked away for the tiny rascals.

That is how the morning went, and when it was time to leave there was the regular reading; the bowed heads in prayer; the feeling that they were all better friends than ever before.

The fog did not lift all day. Instead it hung heavy and clammy close to the water in spite of the sun's best efforts.

Not wishing to be caught in it after dark, we pulled anchor after a hasty lunch and started off across the straits.

The rock and light were scarcely visible except as shadowy forms on our port side as we slipped by them. The foghorn boomed and bellowed as we groped our way out of the pass. We tooted our whistle as a parting call to our friends and were answered with shouts from the youngsters standing on the rock.

Hour upon hour we crept along in the fog. It was so dense that its moisture would accumulate on the rigging and anchor, to drip off in little droplets all day long.

While pushing our way along like this the Skipper suddenly thought he heard the blast of a whistle coming faintly through the fog. He threw back the throttle and swung the ship hard over to starboard.

Out of the fog on our port side churned a giant packer, scarcely visible herself in the comingled colours of her grey and white superstructure. She was going full bore—trusting herself to the radar sweep which swung steadily, though ominously, above her pilothouse. Obviously her radar had not picked us up, for had the Skipper not swung "Messenger III" off course, we would have had a full head-on collision. As it was, so close did she pass by that her crew were able to call across to us quite readily: "Is there anything we can do for you?"

Just about dusk we finally pulled into a little harbour on an Island that stood out to sea with black headlands and timbered ridges.

It had been a fatiguing day, fighting fog all the way, but these men were far from through. Scarcely had they tied up at the dock, before the Missionary went ashore to enquire at the little general store about various families on the Island. There he made arrangements to visit two widows in their respective homes that night.

Meanwhile the Skipper slipped on some hiking boots and invited me to go up the trail with him. Under his arm he carried a bundle of "Shantyman" papers.

We tramped along the gravel road that wound across the Island. The fog still clung to the trees. The moisture dripped from the vegetation and all the forest gave off the dank aroma of decaying vegetation and rotting leaves.

We stopped at a home which doubled as the Island post office. There enough papers were deposited for every family on the Island. The Skipper chatted a wee while with the postmistress, then we tramped on into the dusk to another home.

Here the man and his wife, both of them rather recluses, who dabbled much in philosophy and higher learning, sat in the dimness of their log house, watching the dripping trees.

When the Skipper knocked on the door it was opened furtively. Then there rang out the same old cheerful welcome—and we went in to sit by the fire and share a cup of coffee.

God's Spirit was in our conversation, for soon it led to Eternal Truths and the verities of God's Word. Under the golden glow of the oil lamp we talked of Him who came to give us Life, who gave Himself that we might live. The couple listened attentively and earnestly. In fact, that night they were not far from the Kingdom of God.

We took our leave and tramped back to the boat for supper. The Missionary had been busy with the stove and the fragrance of delicious food met us as we scrambled aboard.

The meal over, the Missionary hastened off to the first widow's home. She had two teen-age children, both with problems common to their years.

There in quietness and gentleness he led them into God's Word, directing them to the source of all wisdom and comfort. What a blessed, blessed way this was to live.

Meanwhile the Skipper and I slipped down to a nearby bay

and there gathered a bucketful of fat, sweet oysters that would augment our larder on board. I had never seen oysters growing in such size or profusion as in that cove where we gathered them that night. Some were so large we carried them stacked on our arms like slabs of firewood.

After this little sortie we met with the Missionary in the home of the second widow lady. She was a young vivacious person, who a short time before had lost both her husband and son in a stormy sea. Now, with only one child left to her, she was trying to salvage something from life with her store, her dogs, and her drink.

I listened in wonderment as she harangued the Shanty Boys with her tales of bravado and high living. But they were not readily abashed, instead they parried her stories with colourful tales of their own, gradually drawing around to the place where they were able to talk gently to her of the goodness of God. When we left, the Missionary asked if he might commit her to the keeping of God, the Bishop and the Shepherd of her soul. To this she assented. Thus another friend had been won; the Shantymen simply had to be "all things to all men."

Again it was late when the light on "Messenger III" went out that night. Again long before dawn the men were up once more. To my astonishment I went out on deck to discover that the Skipper was already out on the dock, helping the recluse we had visited the night before, loading goods in his van to be delivered to the widow's store up the road.

Tireless—tireless workers! Always ready with helping hands!

Is it any marvel these men are loved as they are, up and down the coast? Do we wonder that the love of God is so freely expressed through them to others?

Again we loosed our lines after breakfast and headed north toward another lonely island. The fog was lifting a little and visibility had increased to a mile or more. This day we made better time and good speed winding our way through treacherous channels and narrow openings in the island coast.

By mid-morning we pulled into a tiny hole-in-the-wall scarcely wide enough to swing "Messenger III" around. There we dropped anchor, and hardly had the anchor chain stopped clattering over the bow, when we heard the sound of small boats coming toward us.

Several lads came churning out of a tiny rock-girt bay to greet us. Their clothes were tattered, their boats were beaten up, but wide grins creased their faces. Soon we three bundled ourselves in with them and together we went ashore towards an ancient weather-beaten house that stood upon the bank.

Here, alone, on an eight-hundred-acre island lived a man and his wife with their eleven children. The oldest was a girl of about sixteen, the youngest a babe in arms. For a living the father beach-combed a few logs; shot deer or wild sheep; and collected his family allowance.

It impressed me as a Robinson Crusoe sort of existence with twentieth century overtones. Back of the drab, grey house an old orchard of apples, pears and plums ran wild to unpruned wood. In the meadow alders and young willows were leading the forest back across the fields again. Here a couple of Jersey cows grazed in splendid isolation.

The family insisted we stay to lunch. It was a hearty meal quite unlike any combination I had ever tried before. Boiled beans, stinging nettle greens, all soaked in cream. Then preserved fruit from glass jars, smothered in whipped cream.

After the meal we were invited to sit in the front room—whose sole appointments comprised a broken rocking chair and one 3″ × 12″ plank that passed for a chesterfield.

This was raw, primitive poverty—yet in the face of it the youngsters had bright eyes, ruddy cheeks, and high spirits. In his own inimitable manner the Skipper soon had an armful of young ones from whom he was trying hard to coax one or two tunes.

While we were there, the log boom, where the father held his salvaged logs, had broken loose. In a flash the four older boys, none more than twelve years old, rushed down and leaped into their boats. In veteran style they pushed, pulled, and dragged the logs back into place, while the indifferent dad squatted on the bank sucking on a straw.

"The poor ye shall have always with you!"

This is the thought that coursed through my mind. None of these folks had ever made a commitment to Christ. But when they took us back to the boat the Skipper and the Missionary hauled out a barrel of used clothing and man-handled it over the side into one of their decrepit boats. Before the winter had blown herself out with her vicious winds and driving snow, they would probably be thanking God "Messenger III" had called.

On and on we ran, up a long arm of the sea that twisted its way back into the heartland of the coastal mountains.

Late that night we saw the lights of a small logging camp perched on a shelf of land at the water's edge. We moved in towards the dock, using the searchlight to guide us through the inky darkness.

By this time I was weary with the steady pace. The late nights too were telling. Though I am some twenty years younger than either of these men I rolled into my bunk early that night after writing up my notes. But for them there was still work to do.

Once more they went ashore and that night visited in the home of the camp caretaker. There Christ's invitation was extended to the folks and once more the old, old story of Jesus and His love was poured out to empty, hungry hearts.

A blow had come up in the night, and the ever-alert Skipper had been out and changed the lines on "Messenger III." I slept right through it without knowing anything was amiss. Such is the care of the Skipper for his ship.

The next day, all day, it teemed with rain as only it can rain on the coast. The overcast settled down to a solid cloud cover only a few hundred feet above the sea. The hills around us were indigo-blue with a colour so sombre a man's spirits shrank up inside him cringing from the depressing gloom outside. The water was grey, sullen, and sad with a million drops beating its breast in anguish.

On we churned our way through this dim-lit, half-water, half-sky world of weird fantasy. We were searching for a children's camp where it was known a lonely caretaker and his wife had to live alone all winter.

Finally we found it perched on a finger of rock that jutted from the base of a granite cliff. Above the camp, high on the mountainside a white waterfall cascaded down in plunging fury to the sea. Everything, everywhere, was wet; soaked; sodden and grey. The shakes on the buildings and the limbs on the trees were grey with lichens. Moss and slime adhered to every plank and piece of wood more than a year old. Here water and mist and fog and rain and clouds combined to reduce anything not green and growing to a grey mouldering mass.

In this world we found a solitary man and woman sticking out the long dull winter for Christ's sake . . . because this same spot in summer was alive and vibrant with the voices of hundreds of young people . . . all of it part of the price of the Christian message.

Here there was a firsthand glimpse into that precious comradeship that lies between all those who love the Lord. It was wonderful to feel the warmth, the cheer, the encouragement in God which our unexpected visit brought to this home.

When we left, a lonely man and woman stood at the shore, waving hands that also held handkerchiefs to wipe away a few hot tears.

That is just what the Shantymen mean to so many people in the lonely outposts of the coast.

That day the Skipper expressed a deep desire for a fresh feed of cod. He loves his fish. We had been feeding sumptuously on oysters prepared to perfection by the Missionary. But a fine fat cod would make a nice change.

We had not been travelling long when we spotted a fish boat ahead of us. The Skipper drew alongside. Scarcely had he pulled open the wheelhouse door when the fisherman looked up and recognized him. At once a flashing smile lit his face: "Would you like fresh fish?"

Almost before the Skipper could give an answer two beautiful Alaska cod were flung up on our foredeck.

The fisherman could not tarry. He was in the midst of hauling in his cod lines. But the pause was long enough to exchange warm greetings and supply him with a fresh "Shantyman" paper to read when he rested that night.

The Missionary, with the practiced ease of a veteran, cleaned and filleted the two beautiful fish in short order. His work on the deck attracted scores of immaculate white-winged gulls that drifted over us as we cruised along.

That night the Skipper gorged himself on fresh Alaska cod— a dish fit for a king.

After dinner the three of us made our way to the little chapel in the village. Immediately old friends crowded around the men and they were invited to take a part in the service. Standing there in their rough sea clothes, there poured from their hearts that warmth and love for God which can only come from hearts in tune with Himself.

The next day we were to start back towards where I had boarded the boat. But before we left the Shanty Boys visited a number of homes in the village. Here there was a new pastor who needed to be encouraged in the work; there was a young couple with two beautiful daughters who seemed thrilled to see their old friends once more; here was a rough logger and his wife who by hard slugging and trust in God had hewed out a fine home on this western shore. How proud they were for the Shantymen to see what had been achieved since their last visit.

And now the trip was behind us and we were on the last leg of the journey. For me this had not been a new revelation, for I had sailed with these men before . . . but it had been a refreshment to my spirit once more to be with men so utterly dedicated to their Master.

Standing at the rail of "Messenger III"—waching her white wake stretch out across the Pacific—one persistent question hovered relentlessly in my mind regarding these Shanty Boys—

ARE THERE OTHERS WHO WILL FOLLOW THEIR FOOTSTEPS? THOSE WHO WILL PROVE TO A WAITING WORLD—THE UNCHANGING FAITHFULNESS OF GOD?

Date Due

FEB 0 6 1991			

CPSIA information can be obtained
at www.ICGtesting.com
Printed in the USA
BVHW062241220122
626943BV00002B/89